KU-441-326

THE ROUGH GUIDE TO

ANTIGUA
AND BARBUDA

by Adam Vaitilingam

WITHDRAWN FROM
ISLINGTON LIBRARIES

**ROUGH
GUIDES**

We set out to do something different when the first Rough Guide was published in 1982. Mark Ellingham, just out of university, was travelling in Greece. He brought along the popular guides of the day, but found they were all lacking in some way. They were either strong on ruins and museums but went on for pages without mentioning a beach or taverna. Or they were so conscious of the need to save money that they lost sight of Greece's cultural and historical significance. Also, none of the books told him anything about Greece's contemporary life – its politics, its culture, its people, and how they lived.

So with no job in prospect, Mark decided to write his own guidebook, one which aimed to provide practical information that was second to none, detailing the best beaches and the hottest clubs and restaurants, while also giving hard-hitting accounts of every sight, both famous and obscure, and providing up-to-the-minute information on contemporary culture. It was a guide that encouraged independent travellers to find the best of Greece, and was a great success, getting shortlisted for the Thomas Cook travel guide award, and encouraging Mark, along with three friends, to expand the series.

The Rough Guide list grew rapidly and the letters flooded in, indicating a much broader readership than had been anticipated, but one which uniformly appreciated the Rough Guide mix of practical detail and humour, irreverence and enthusiasm. Things haven't changed. The same four friends who began the series are still the caretakers of the Rough Guide mission today: to provide the most reliable, up-to-date and entertaining information to independent-minded travellers of all ages, on all budgets.

We now publish more than 150 titles and have offices in London and New York. The travel guides are written and researched by a dedicated team of more than 100 authors, based in Britain, Europe, the USA and Australia. We have also created a unique series of phrasebooks to accompany the travel series, along with an acclaimed series of music guides, and a best-selling pocket guide to the Internet and World Wide Web. We also publish comprehensive travel information on our Web site: **www.roughguides.com**

Help us update

We've gone to a lot of trouble to ensure that this Rough Guide is as up to date and accurate as possible. However, things do change and all suggestions, comments and corrections are much appreciated; we'll send a copy of the next edition (or any other Rough Guide if you prefer) for the best letters.

Please mark letters "**Rough Guide Antigua and Barbuda Update**" and send to:

Rough Guides, 62–70 Shorts Gardens, London WC2H 9AH, or Rough Guides, 4th Floor, 345 Hudson St, New York, NY 10014.

Or send email to: mail@roughguides.co.uk

Online updates about this book can be found on Rough Guides' Web site (see opposite)

The author

Adam Vaitilingam is a barrister and freelance writer who lived in the West Indies from 1989 to 1993. He is also the author of the Rough Guide to Barbados and co-author of the Rough Guide to Jamaica, and now lives in Devon.

Acknowledgements

Adam: Thanks to Chris and the guys at Long Bay and everyone at Chickies.

Readers' letters

Many thanks to the readers of the first edition who took the time to write in with their comments and suggestions:
Frank Ankawi, Veronica Chamberlain, Rob Church, Caroline Hart, Shaun Howard, Leon Jefferson, Barry Phillips, Richard Skills, Jen Turner, Clare Wood and the many folks who contacted us via email but preferred to remain anonymous.

CONTENTS

Map list   viii

Introduction   ix

Basics   1

Getting there   3

Getting around   15

Visas and red tape   19

Health and insurance   21

Information and maps   24

Money and costs   26

Communications and the media   29

Festivals, events and public holidays   31

Shopping   33

Drugs, trouble and harassment   34

The Guide   37

1   St John's and around   39

2   From Runaway Bay to Half Moon Bay   51

3   Falmouth and English Harbour   58

4   The West Coast   71

5   Barbuda and Redonda   77

Listings   87

6   Accommodation   89

7   Eating and drinking   103

8   Music and nightlife   118

9   Sports   123

10   Directory   134

Contexts   137

A brief history of Antigua   139

Cricket   147

Books   151

Index   154

MAP LIST

1 The Caribbean   x

Maps at back of book

2 Antigua

3 St John's

4 Runaway Bay & Dickenson Bay

5 Falmouth & English Harbour

6 Barbuda

MAP SYMBOLS

═══	Major road	⌓	Cave
═══	Minor road	▲	Peak
───	Waterway	✈	Airport
⸸	Church	◼	Accommodation
✉	Post office	◉	Places to eat and drink
ⓘ	Information office	⸬	Beach
♛	Castle	▦	Park

Introduction

Famous for its beaches and its cricket players, tiny **Antigua** is rapidly becoming one of the Caribbean's most popular destinations. Quiet, unvisited and little-known just a generation ago, the country has taken full advantage of the publicity gained from its independence in 1981 – and the remarkable success of its cricketers since then – to push its name into the big league of West Indian tourism alongside Barbados and Jamaica.

Antigua's early European settlers came from Britain in the sixteenth century. They brought African slaves to clear the native vegetation and plant sugarcane: for centuries, the island was little more than a giant sugar factory, producing sugar and rum to send home to an increasingly sweet-toothed mother country. Around Antigua, the tall brick chimneys of a hundred deserted and decaying sugar mills bear witness to that long colonial era. Today, though, it is tourism that drives the country's economy; dozens of **hotels** and **restaurants** have sprung up around the coast-line, there's a smart new airport, and people offer **boat** and **catamaran cruises** and **scuba diving** and **snorkelling** trips to the island's fabulous coral reefs.

If all you want to do is crash out on a **beach** for a week or two, you'll find Antigua hard to beat. The island is dotted with superb patches of sand - look out for **Dickenson**

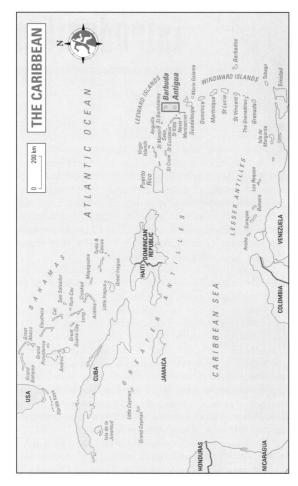

Bay in the northwest, **Half Moon Bay** in the east and **Rendezvous Beach** in the south - and, while the nightlife is generally pretty quiet, there are plenty of great places to eat and drink. But however lazy you're feeling, it's worth making the effort to get out and see some of the country. The superbly restored naval dockyard and the crumbling forts around **English Harbour** and **Shirley Heights** are as impressive as any historic site in the West Indies, and there are lots of other little nuggets to explore, including the capital, **St John's**, with its tiny museum and colourful quayside, and the old sugar estate at **Betty's Hope**. And, if you're prepared to do a bit of walking, you'll find some superb **hikes** that will take you out to completely deserted parts of the island.

Antigua's sister island **Barbuda** feels a world apart from its increasingly developed neighbour, even though it's just fifteen minutes away by plane. Despite its spectacular beaches and coral reefs, tourism is very low-key; for the island's tiny population, the pace of life seems to have changed little over the generations, and fishing is still the main occupation. Even if you can only manage a day-trip, you'll find it thoroughly repays the effort involved in organizing a tour.

When to go

For many visitors, Antigua's leading attraction is its **tropical climate**: hot and sunny all year round. The weather is at its best during the high season, from mid-December to mid-April, with rainfall low and the heat tempered by cooling trade winds. Things can get noticeably hotter during the summer and, particularly in September and October, the humidity can become oppressive. September is also the most threatening month of the annual hurricane season, which runs officially from June 1 to October 31, though it's

WHEN TO GO

ANTIGUA'S CLIMATE

	AVERAGE DAILY TEMP °F		AVERAGE DAILY TEMP °C		AVERAGE MONTHLY RAINFALL	
	MAX	MIN	MAX	MIN	IN	MM
Jan	82	70	28	21	4.8	122
Feb	83	70	28	21	3.4	86
March	85	70	29	21	4.4	112
April	86	72	30	22	3.5	89
May	88	74	31	23	3.8	97
June	88	75	31	24	4.4	112
July	87	75	31	24	6.1	155
Aug	88	75	31	24	7.2	183
Sept	89	74	32	23	6.6	168
Oct	87	74	31	23	7.7	196
Nov	85	73	29	23	7.1	180
Dec	83	72	28	22	5.5	140

worth bearing in mind that, on average, the big blows only hit about once a decade.

As you'd expect, prices and crowds are at their peak during high season, when the main attractions and beaches can get pretty packed. Outside this period everywhere is a little quieter, flight and accommodation prices come down (often dramatically) and you'll find more scope for negotiation on other items.

BASICS

Getting there   3

Getting around   15

Visas and red tape   19

Health and insurance   21

Information and maps   24

Money and costs   26

Communications and the media   29

Festivals, events and public holidays   31

Shopping   33

Drugs, trouble and harassment   34

Getting there

By far the easiest and cheapest way to get to Antigua is by **air**. Indeed, besides the occasional cruise, which typically only dock in Antigua for a matter of hours, an international flight is just about your only option. Regardless of where you buy your ticket, fares will depend on the season. These vary from airline to airline, but mid-December to mid-April is generally classified as **high season**, and the rest of the year **low season**. In July and August, however, mid-priced shoulder-season fares come into play.

Apart from special promotions, the cheapest published fare is usually an **Apex ticket**, although you typically have to book and pay at least 21 days in advance, and you tend to get penalized if you change your schedule.

You can normally cut costs further by going through a consolidator or discount agent, who may also offer **student and youth fares** and a range of other services such as travel insurance, car rental and tours. Penalties for changing your plans can be stiff, however.

A further possibility is the **internet**, where many airlines and discount travel Web sites offer you the opportunity to book your tickets online, cutting out the costs of agents and middlemen; besides the airlines' own sites, try out ⓦwww.ebookers.com, ⓦwww.travelocity, ⓦwww.expedia .com and ⓦwww.cheapflights.com.

A **package holiday** can offer excellent value, and often works out much cheaper than arranging separate flights, transfers and accommodation yourself. There are all kinds of deals available, depending on whether you opt for an all-inclusive (hotel room plus all meals), room only, or self-catering option (usually a hotel room with simple cooking facilities).

GETTING THERE FROM BRITAIN AND IRELAND

Most British and Irish visitors to Antigua are on some form of package tour that includes a charter flight direct to the island. This is the simplest way of going and, even if you plan to travel independently, a seat on a charter is normally the cheapest too. But charters do have their drawbacks, especially if your plans don't fit into their usual two-week straitjacket. As an alternative, a couple of airlines offer direct scheduled flights from London, and you can find similar fares with other carriers that require a stopover in the USA. There are no direct flights from Ireland to Antigua, but there are good connections via London or via New York and Miami (see "Getting There from the USA and Canada", p.7).

There are no direct flights to Barbuda; for details on getting there from Antigua, see chapter 5 of the *Guide*.

FARES, FLIGHTS AND AIRPASSES

Most of the discount and specialist travel agents listed on p.6 can quote **fares** on scheduled and charter flights, although some (including STA and usit CAMPUS which specialize in youth and **student fares**) only quote for scheduled flights. Other useful sources of information include the ads in London's *Time Out* magazine and the travel pages in the *Observer* and other Sunday newspapers.

Teletext and Ceefax are also worth a look, as is your local travel agent.

British Airways, Virgin and BWIA fly from London, with return fares starting at between £400 and £500 in low season, reaching £700–800 in high season. It's sometimes cheaper, if less convenient, to change planes in the US, normally in Miami (see p.8). Delta, Virgin, British Airways and American Airlines all fly from London to Miami, with fares as little as £200–250 during the low season.

Charter operators Air 2000 fly from London Gatwick once per week (Wed). They can be cheaper than scheduled flights, but tend to arrive and depart at antisocial hours, and there is little or no flexibility once the ticket is booked. Fares start at around £200 during low season, rising to £400+ in high season. Most charter flights are for a fortnight, though you can also find charters for one or three weeks.

Airlines

Aer Lingus in London
ⓣ020/8899 4747, outside London ⓣ0845/973 7747, in Republic of Ireland ⓣ01/705 3333 or 844 4777,
ⓦwww.aerlingus.ie

Air 2000 ⓣ0870/757 2757,
ⓦwww.unijet.com

American Airlines ⓣ0845/778 9789, ⓦwww.aa.com

British Airways ⓣ0845/773 3377, in Republic of Ireland ⓣ0800/626 747,
ⓦwww.british-airways.com

BWIA ⓣ020/8577 1100,
ⓦwww.bwee.com

Delta Air Lines
ⓣ0800/414767, in Northern Ireland ⓣ028/9048 0526, in Republic of Ireland
ⓣ1800/414767,
ⓦwww.delta-air.com

Virgin Atlantic
ⓣ01293/747747, in Republic of Ireland ⓣ01/873 3388,
ⓦwww.virgin-atlantic.com

GETTING THERE FROM BRITAIN AND IRELAND

Discount agents

Budget Travel Dublin ⓣ01/661 1403

Council Travel ⓣ020/7437 7767,ⓦ www.counciltravel.com

Flightbookers ⓣ020/7757 2444, ⓦ www.ebookers.com

Joe Walsh Tours Dublin ⓣ01/872 2555 or 676 3053, Cork ⓣ021/277959, ⓦ www.joewalshtours.ie

The London Flight Centre ⓣ020/7244 6411, ⓦ www.topdecktravel.co.uk

New Look Travel ⓣ020/8965 8212

Newmont Travel ⓣ020/7254 6546

Redfern Travel ⓣ01274/733551

STA Travel ⓣ0870/160 6070, ⓦ www.statravel.co.uk

Trailfinders ⓣ020/7628 7628, in Republic of Ireland ⓣ01/677 7888, ⓦ www.trailfinders.com

usit CAMPUS ⓣ0870/240 1010 ⓦ www.usitcampus.co.uk

usit NOW Belfast ⓣ028/9032 7111, Dublin ⓣ01/602 1777 or 677 8117, Cork ⓣ021/270900, Derry ⓣ028/7137 1888, ⓦ www.usit.ie

PACKAGES AND TOURS

Most **packages** on offer from the UK are for two weeks, and you may have to shop around to find a one-week or three-week deal. Obviously, it's worth getting a selection of brochures before you choose and checking the Web sites, particularly Virgin Holidays and First Choice. All-inclusive packages start at around £700 per person for a week, £1000 for a fortnight, based on double occupancy, while room-only and self-catering deals start at around £500 per person for a week, £600 for a fortnight, again based on two people sharing. All deals include the flight and transfers from airport to hotel.

Typical package offerings include a three-star all-inclusive with First Choice (between £1100 and £1500) and a four-

GETTING THERE FROM BRITAIN AND IRELAND

star all-inclusive with Virgin Holidays (between £1200 and £1600), all prices per person for a fortnight including flights and based on two adults sharing.

A handful of tour operators offer **specialized tours** based, for example, around getting married or catching the West Indies cricket season. And if you want to see Antigua for a day, you could do worse than a Caribbean cruise; these start at around £1000, including a return flight to the embarkation point in Miami.

Specialist package and tour operators

Airtours ☎ 0870/241 2567, Ⓦ www.airtours.co.uk

Caribtours ☎ 020/7751 0660

Cosmos Travel ☎ 020/8464 3444, Ⓦ www.cosmos-holidays.co.uk

First Choice ☎ 0870/750 0001, Ⓦ www.firstchoice.co.uk

Hayes and Jarvis ☎ 0870/898 9890, Ⓦ www.hayes-jarvis.com

Kuoni Travel ☎ 01306/742888, Ⓦ www.kuoni.co.uk

Thomas Cook ☎ 0870/566 6222, Ⓦ www.thomascook.co.uk

Thomson Holidays ☎ 0870/550 2555

Tropical Places ☎ 01342/825123

Virgin Holidays ☎ 01293/456789, Ⓦ www.virginholidays.co.uk

GETTING THERE FROM THE USA AND CANADA

The most obvious way of getting to Antigua from North America is **by air**. There are few cheap flights to Antigua, however, and the airlines usually don't offer special student rates or airpasses. Nor does the Caribbean fit too well into a round-the-world (RTW) itinerary. For more leisurely transport, several **cruise ships** call at the island, and it is even possible to sail there by **yacht** from Florida.

FARES AND FLIGHTS

The following are typical high/low season APEX fares, departing midweek, from US/Canadian cities to VC Bird International Airport in Antigua: New York City (US$600/470); Atlanta (US$760/705); Chicago (US$800 /745); Los Angeles (US$950/900); Miami (US$575/515); Toronto (CAN$875/725). American Airlines offers the best fares and most comprehensive schedule from the United States to Antigua; all of their flights connect either through Miami or San Juan, Puerto Rico. BWIA flies nonstop to Antigua from New York City and Miami, while Continental has three weekly nonstop flights out of Newark, New Jersey.

Air Canada offers the best fares out of Toronto, although they only fly to Antigua on Saturdays; American Airlines has a wider range of options at competitive prices. BWIA's direct flight from Toronto, which leaves once a week, is also good value. Getting from Vancouver to Antigua is a challenge since an overnight stay is usually required to catch a flight from Toronto or one of the US gateways.

Another solution is to fly to San Juan, Puerto Rico and then on to Antigua; American Eagle flies to San Juan non-stop from LA, Dallas, Chicago, Baltimore/Washington Dulles, Miami and Kennedy/Newark. Vancouver via New York City to San Juan, for example, costs around CAN$697 year round. Flights from Chicago are US$802/542 and from New York City US$450/262 in high/low season. From San Juan to Antigua is about US$190 round-trip, year round, though cheaper specials are frequent.

Airlines

Air Canada ☎ 1-800/263-0882
in Canada, ☎ 1-800/776-3000
in US, ⓦ www.aircanada.ca

American Airlines
☎ 1-800/433-7300,
ⓦ www.aa.com

American Eagle ☎ 1-800/433-
7300, ⓦ www.aa.com

BWIA ☎ 1-800/538-2942,
ⓦ www.bwee.com

Continental Airlines
☎ 1-800/525-0280 domestic,
☎ 1-800/231-0856
international, ⓦ www
.continental.com

Discount travel agents and consolidators

Council Travel ☎ 1-800/226-
8624, ⓦ www.counciltravel
.com

STA Travel ☎ 1-800/777-0112,
ⓦ www.sta-travel.com

Travel CUTS ☎ 1-800/667-
2887 Canada only or
☎ 416/979-2406,
ⓦ www.travelcuts.com

Worldtek Travel ☎ 1-800/243-
1723, ⓦ www.worldtek.com

PACKAGES AND TOURS

- -

Although flights from North America to Antigua can be reasonably priced, you can sometimes find an even less-expensive alternative with a **vacation package**. Most cover the airfare, transfers, accommodation and airport taxes, and can include meals. Prices start from US$880, leaving from New York or Miami (BWIA Vacations), for seven nights in low season, and generally hover around US$1500 for a two-week stay.

Although phone numbers are given overleaf, you're better off making tour reservations through your local travel agent, who will make all the phone calls and arrange flights, insurance and the like at no extra cost.

Tour operators

Air Canada Vacations
  ℡ 1-800/774-8993
Alken Tours ℡ 1-800/221-6686
  or 718/856-7711
American Airlines Vacations
  ℡ 1-800/321-2121
BWIA Vacations ℡ 1-800/780-
  5501 or 718/520-8100
Friendly Holidays ℡ 1-800
  /456-7754

Inter Island Tours ℡ 1-800
  /245-3434
Tour Host International
  ℡ 1-800/THE-HOST or
  212/953-7910
TourScan Inc ℡ 1-800/962-
  2080 or 203/655-8091,
  ⓦ www.tourscan.com
Travel Impressions ℡ 1-800
  /284-0044

BY SEA

If you plan to **yacht** to Antigua, the US Coast Guard in Miami will steer you in the right direction (℡ 305/535-4470), or you can call US Sailing (℡ 1-800/US-SAIL-1 or 401/683-0800). If you'd rather go on a bit larger vessel, **cruise ships** make frequent calls into the port at St John's. The fares quoted below are for **low season** (see p.3) seven-day cruises in single-person/double-occupancy "inside" (no ocean views) cabins, and are exclusive of port charges which add an extra US$110 to US$150. The cruises stop only once in Antigua and leave from San Juan, Puerto Rico unless otherwise noted.

Cruise lines

Celebrity Cruises ℡ 1-800
/437-3111, ⓦ www.celebrity-cruises.com; from US$899
Cunard ℡ 1-800/221-4770,
ⓦ www.cunardline.com; from US$5670 for a sixteen-day

cruise from Lisbon to Miami or seven days on a luxury 116-person "yacht" out of St Thomas from US$6750
Holland American Line
  ℡ 1-800/426-0327 or 206/

281-3535,
ⓦ www.hollandamerica.com;
from US$1592 for a ten-day
cruise starting in Fort
Lauderdale
Norwegian Cruise Line
ⓣ 1-800/327-7030,
ⓦ www.ncl.com; from US$649
Royal Caribbean International
ⓣ 1-800/327-6700,
ⓦ www.royalcaribbean.com;
from US$699 including port
charges

Royal Olympic ⓣ 1-800
/368-3888,
ⓦ www.royalolympiccruises
.com; fourteen-day cruises
from Fort Lauderdale to Brazil
or vice versa starting at
US$1977
Windjammer ⓣ 1-800
/327-2601,
ⓦ www.windjammer.com; six-
day round-trip cruise starting
and ending in Antigua from
US$875

GETTING THERE FROM AUSTRALIA AND NEW ZEALAND

Antigua is no bargain destination from Australasia. There are no direct flights from Australia or New Zealand, so you'll have to take a flight to one of the main US gateway airports, and pick up onward connections from there. Generally, the least expensive and most straightforward routes are via Miami, from where there are regular flights to St John's. If you're planning to see Antigua as part of a longer trip, **round-the-world** (RTW) tickets are worth considering, and are usually better value than a simple return flight. Whatever kind of ticket you're after, first call should be one of the **specialist travel agents** listed on p.14, which can fill you in on all the latest fares and any special offers. If you're a **student** or **under 26**, you may be able to undercut some of the prices given here; STA is a good place to start.

FARES AND AIRPASSES

- -

All the fares quoted below are for travel during **low or shoulder seasons**, and exclude airport taxes; flying at peak times (primarily Dec to mid-Jan and mid-May to end-Aug) can add substantially to these prices.

The best fares you're likely to find are the Air New Zealand, United and Qantas regular services to Los Angeles, with connecting flights to Miami flying American Airlines or United: return fares to Miami cost around A\$2000 from the **eastern states**, rising to A\$2250 from **Western Australia**. From **New Zealand**, the same airlines fly to Los Angeles, with connections on to Miami; through fares to Miami start at NZ\$2000.

Onward flights from Miami to **St John's** cost around A\$450/NZ\$500 return, flying with BWIA. American Airlines also operate flights from Chicago and Atlanta, via San Juan, at similar prices. (See "Getting there from the USA and Canada" for more on connections from North America.)

RTW TICKETS

- -

Given these fares and routings, **round-the-world tickets** that take in one of the gateway airports in the United States are worth considering, especially if you have the time to make the most of a few stopovers. There are plenty of options, depending on where else you want to go, but tickets start at around A\$1750/NZ\$2250.

Airlines

Air New Zealand Australia
ⓣ13 2476, New Zealand

ⓣ0800/737 000 or 09/357
3000, ⓦwww.airnz.com

American Airlines Australia
ⓣ 1300/650 747,
New Zealand ⓣ 09/309 0735
or 0800/887 997,
ⓦ www.aa.com
BWIA International Airways
ⓣ 02/9285 6811,
ⓦ www.bwiacaribbean.com
Delta Air Lines, Australia
ⓣ 02/9251 3211 or 800/500
992, New Zealand ⓣ 09/379

3370 or 0800/440 876,
ⓦ www.delta-air.com
Qantas Australia ⓣ 13 1313,
New Zealand ⓣ 09/357 8900
or 0800/808 767,
ⓦ www.qantas.com.au
United Airlines Australia
ⓣ 13 1777, New Zealand
ⓣ 09/379 3800,
ⓦ www.ual.com

PACKAGES AND TOURS

Package holidays from Australia and New Zealand to Antigua are few and far between, and many specialists simply act as **agents** for US-based operators, tagging a return flight from Australasia on to the total cost. **Cruises** account for the largest sector of the market: most depart from Miami, and because prices are based on US dollar amounts, they fluctuate with the exchange rate, but to give some idea, all-inclusive three-day cruises start from A$650, while seven-day cruises cost upwards of A$1000. The luxury end of the market is also catered for by Caribbean Destinations, which offers **resort-** and **villa-based holidays** as well as cruises, with a choice of accommodation on Antigua. Prices start around A$3500 for fourteen days (based on twin-share accommodation and low-season airfares from Australia), and rising inexorably.

None of the adventure-tour operators venture to Antigua; for independent travellers, the cheapest way to visit the Caribbean is as part of a round-the-world or American holiday.

Travel agents

Anywhere Travel ⓣ 02/9663
0411 or 018/401 014,
ⓔ anywhere@ozemail.com.au
Budget Travel New Zealand
ⓣ 09/366 0061 or 0800/808
040
Destinations Unlimited New
Zealand ⓣ 09/373 4033
Flight Centre Australia
ⓣ 02/9235 3522 or for nearest
branch ⓣ 13 1600, New
Zealand ⓣ 09/358 4310,
ⓦ www.flightcentre.com.au
Northern Gateway Australia
ⓣ 08/8941 1394,
ⓔ oztravel@norgate.com.au

STA Travel Australia ⓣ 13 1776
or 1300/360 960, New Zealand
ⓣ 09/309 0458 or 366 6673,
ⓦ www.statravel.com.au
Student Uni Travel Australia
ⓣ 02/9232 8444,
ⓔ Australia@backpackers.net
Thomas Cook Australia ⓣ 13
1771 or 1800/801 002, New
Zealand ⓣ 09/379 3920,
ⓦ www.thomascook.com.au
Trailfinders Australia
ⓣ 02/9247 7666
usit BEYOND New Zealand
ⓣ 09/379 4224 or 0800/788
336, ⓦ www.usitbeyond.co.nz

Specialist agents and tour operators

Caribbean Destinations
Australia ⓣ 03/9614 7144,
ⓦ www.caribbeanislands.com
.au
Creative Tours ⓣ 02/9836
2111

Wiltrans Australia ⓣ 02/9255
0899 or 1800/251 174,
ⓦ www.maupintours.com

Getting around

A lot of people come to Antigua, make straight for their hotel and spend the next fortnight lying on the beach. For those who want to tour around and see the island, though, there are a variety of options.

Speedy and inexpensive buses run to certain parts of the island, particularly between St John's and English Harbour on the south coast, although none go to the big tourist area of Dickenson Bay and Runaway Bay. If you want to tour around, you're invariably better off renting a **car** for a couple of days – though this isn't cheap. If you just want to make the odd excursion or short trip, it can work out cheaper to hire **taxis**.

BY BUS

The public transport system in Antigua is patchy, with **buses** offering fast, frequent and cheap service between St John's and English Harbour, via the centre of the island,

---

GETTING TO AND FROM THE AIRPORT

There is no bus service to and from V.C. Bird International Airport. There are numerous **car rental** outlets at the airport, while **taxis** – arranged through the dispatch desk – cost around US$6 to Dickenson Bay or US$25 to English Harbour.

and less frequent service to Parham and Willikies on the east coast (from where it's a fifteen-minute walk to the Long Bay beach). There is no service to the tourist strip of Runaway Bay and Dickenson Bay on the northwest coast, nor to the airport. Buses and **minibuses** also run along the west coast between St John's and Old Road, stopping off beside several good beaches and the local hotels en route. They also run out to the Five Islands peninsula. For the south and west coasts, buses and minibuses use the West End bus terminal near the main market in St John's; for the east coast, they use the east terminal near the Recreation Ground.

Few of the buses run to any schedule, often departing only when they are reasonably full. Always ask the driver where he's going and tell him well in advance of where you want to get off. Stops are normally marked, though you'll find that the minivans will usually stop anywhere en route. Few buses run after dark or on Sunday.

BY CAR

Antigua is an easy country to **drive** in; driving is on the left, the roads are mostly good and distances are small. True, signposting is abysmal, but it's hard to get seriously lost – asking passers-by is the best way to get information if you do. In St John's, though, the streets are narrow and poorly lit, so driving there at night is normally best avoided.

Rental prices, however, are fairly high, starting at around US$40 per day, $250 per week. Third-party **insurance** is included in the price; if you don't have a credit card that offers free collision damage insurance, you'll have to pay another US$10–12 per day if you want to cover potential damage to the rental car.

When renting, you'll need to buy a local driving licence for US$20 (valid for three months) and to show a current **licence** from your home country or an international driver's licence. You'll also normally need a **credit card** to make a security deposit. Check the car fully to ensure that every dent, scratch or missing part is inventoried before you set off. When returning the car, don't forget to collect any credit-card deposit slip.

Reliable firms include: Avis (☎ 462 2840), Budget (☎ 462 3009), Dollar (☎ 462 0362), Hertz (☎ 462 4114), Oakland (☎ 462 3021) and Thrifty (☎ 462 9532). Each of these can provide you with a car at the airport or deliver to your hotel.

BY TAXI

Finding a **taxi** in Antigua – identifiable from an H on their numberplates – is easy in St John's, Nelson's Dockyard or at the airport; less straightforward in other areas of the island, where you'll often need to call (or ask your hotel to arrange) for one. Fares are regulated but there are no meters, so make sure that you agree a price before you get into the car. At the airport there is a list of government-approved rates: US$7 to St John's, $6 to Dickenson Bay or Runaway Bay, $25 to English Harbour. If you rent a taxi for a day's sightseeing, expect to pay around US$60–70.

MOTORBIKES AND CYCLING

Since Antigua is so small, and there are few steep inclines, it is ideal **cycling** territory, and bikes can be rented for around US$15 per day, US$70 a week. Hiring a scooter or **motorbike** is just as fun – prices normally start at around US$30 per day, US$150 a week (plus $20 for the local driving permit) – and can be a fantastic way of touring around, though you'll need to watch out for madcap drivers on the main roads. Rental agents for both bikes and motorbikes include Cycle Krazy, St Mary's Street in St John's

(☎462 9253), Paradise Boat Sales at Jolly Harbour (☎460 7125) and Shipwreck in Parham (☎464 7771; they deliver to your hotel, so cost a little more).

TOURS

In case you don't fancy driving, there are a couple of local companies who offer islandwide **sightseeing tours**, either to a set itinerary or customized to your needs. Remember to check whether the price includes entrance fees to the various attractions. Your hotel may also organize tours direct. If you can't get a good price from any of the companies below, you could check with some of the taxi operators listed in the "Directory" on p.136.

Tropikelly Trails (☎461 0383) offer five- to six-hour tours from US$65 including a picnic lunch per person, with trips to Great George Fort, Boggy Peak and a pineapple farm, or

VISITING OTHER ISLANDS

LIAT (☎462 0700) are based in Antigua and run flights to virtually all of the Caribbean islands as well as into Venezuela in South America. Fares start at around US$75 for round-trip flights to nearby Guadeloupe; longer-haul flights start at around US$100, but most will allow you one or more free stopovers en route. Tickets are sold at a multitude of travel agents islandwide. The brand new airline Caribbean Star (☎480 2501) now operates out of Antigua to a number of islands, including Barbados, Dominica, Grenada and St Kitts; costs are similar to LIAT. Carib Airlines (☎462 3147) offer local charters, and can work out cheaper than LIAT for a group of five to nine people. D&J Forwarders (☎773 9766) and Jenny's Tours (☎461 9361) both offer daytrips by ferry (1hr) to Montserrat for US$130 to $150 per person.

TOURS

a half-day tour for US$35. Estate Safari Jeep tours (☎463 4713) offer similar tours, including Betty's Hope sugar plantation, Great George Fort and lunch on the beach, while Antours (☎462 4788) and Bo Tours (☎462 6632) also offer tours to the island's main sights, including English Harbour and Betty's Hope at a similar cost.

For tours to Barbuda, see chapter 5 of the *Guide*.

YACHTING CHARTERS

Charters can be arranged through Sun Yacht Charters (☎460 2615) or Nicholson's Yacht Charters (☎460 1530), both at English Harbour.

Visas and red tape

Citizens of Britain, Ireland, the US, Canada, Australia and New Zealand can enter Antigua without a **visa** and stay for up to six months. You will, however, need a **passport** (valid for at least six months after the date of onward travel) and a return ticket or proof of onward travel. You might also be asked to show that you have sufficient funds to cover your stay; if you can't satisfy the immigration authorities, they have the right to deny you entry. You will also be asked where you intend to stay, though your answer will not of course be binding. There is no fee for entering Antigua, but you will have to pay a US$20/EC$50 **departure tax** when you leave.

ANTIGUAN EMBASSIES AND CONSULATES

Canada 105 Adelaide St W, Suite 1010, Toronto, ON M5H 1P9, ☎ 416/214-9805.

UK 1 Great Russell St, London WC1B 3JY, ☎ 020/7631 4975.

US 3216 New Mexico Ave NW, Washington, DC 20016, ☎ 202/362-5122.

There is no Antiguan embassy or consulate in Ireland, Australia or New Zealand.

FOREIGN EMBASSIES IN ANTIGUA

British High Commission, St John's, ☎ 462 0008.
US Consular Office, English Harbour, ☎ 463 6531.

There are no Canadian or Australian embassies or commissions in Antigua.

VISAS AND RED TAPE

Health and insurance

I f you need medical or dental treatment on the island, you'll find the standard reasonably high. St John's has the 225-bed public **Holberton Hospital** (☎462 0251) on its eastern outskirts, while smaller health centres and clinics are distributed around the island. For an **ambulance**, call ☎462 0251.

Before buying an **insurance policy**, check that you're not already covered. Private health plans typically provide some **overseas medical coverage**, although they are unlikely to pick up the full tab in the event of a mishap. Homeowners' or renters' insurance often covers theft or loss of documents, money and valuables while overseas.

HEALTH

Travelling in Antigua is usually very safe as far as **health** is concerned. Food is invariably well and hygienically prepared and the tap water is safe to drink.

No jabs are needed – the major tropical diseases were eradicated long ago – and you'll find that the only real threat to your physical welfare is the intense **Caribbean**

sun. Many visitors get badly sunburned on the first day and suffer for the rest of the trip – you'll see them peeling around the island. To avoid their fate, it's advisable to wear a strong sun screen at all times; if you're after a tan, start strong and gradually reduce the factor. As for exposure times, 15 minutes a day in the early morning or late afternoon is recommended, if rarely followed; unreconstructed sun-worshippers should at least avoid the heat of the day between 11.30am and 2.30pm. For the sunburned, aloe vera gel is available at the island's pharmacies.

While you're on the beach, steer clear of the **manchineel trees**, recognizable by their shiny green leaves and the small, crab apple-like fruits scattered around on the ground. The fruit is poisonous and, when it rains, the bark gives off a poisonous sap that will cause blisters if it drips on you. The sea, too, poses a handful of threats. Don't worry about the rarely seen sharks or barracudas, which won't spoil your visit, but watch out for spiny black **sea urchins**. They're easily missed if you're walking over a patch of sea grass; if you step on one and can't get the spines out, you'll need medical help. Finally, mosquitoes and tiny sandflies can be an occasional problem, particularly on the beach in late afternoon; take **insect repellent** to keep them at bay.

INSURANCE

Most people will find it essential to take out a good **travel insurance policy** for a trip to Antigua, ideally covering at least medical treatment, theft and loss of baggage. Check first, though, to find out if you already have any coverage. Bank and credit cards (particularly American Express) often have certain levels of medical or other insurance included if you use them to pay for your trip; this can be quite comprehensive, anticipating such mishaps as lost or stolen baggage, missed connections and charter companies going

ROUGH GUIDES TRAVEL INSURANCE

Rough Guides offers its own **travel insurance**, customized for our readers by a leading UK broker and backed by a Lloyds underwriter. It's available for anyone, of any nationality, travelling anywhere in the world.

There are two main Rough Guide insurance plans: **Essential**, for basic, no-frills cover; and **Premier** – with more generous and extensive benefits. Unlike many policies, the Rough Guides schemes are calculated by the day, so if you're travelling for 27 days rather than a month, that's all you pay for. Each plan can also be supplemented with a "Hazardous Activities Premium" if you plan to indulge in sports considered dangerous, such as scuba diving. Rough Guides also does good deals for older travellers, and will insure you up to any age, at prices comparable to SAGA's.

For a **policy quote**, call the Rough Guides Insurance Line on UK freefone ☏ 0800/015 0906, toll-free in the US on 1-866/220-5588, or worldwide on ☏ (+44) 1243/621046. Alternatively, get an online quote at ⓦ www.roughguides.com/insurance.

bust. Similarly, if you have a good "all risks" home insurance policy, it may well cover your possessions against loss or theft even when overseas, and many private medical schemes also cover you when abroad – make sure you know the procedure and the relevant telephone number. If you're planning a trip to mainland South America, make sure that your insurance extends to the region.

In all cases of loss or **theft** of goods, you will have to contact the local police to have a report made out so that your insurer can process the claim; for **medical claims**, you'll need to provide receipts and supporting bills. If you are going to make a claim, make a note of any time period within which you must lodge it, and keep photocopies of everything you send to the insurer.

INSURANCE

Information and maps

Before you leave home, you may want to contact the **Antigua Tourist Office** (ATO) nearest you. Their offices stock plenty of information on the country, including brochures on the main tourist attractions and forthcoming events, and a good road map. Once you're in Antigua, you can get the same information from the ATO office in St John's (see p.40) or from their desk at the airport. Most of the car rental outlets will also provide you with a free map of the island when you rent from them.

Antigua has no detailed listings magazine for music, theatre and other events, though the *Antigua Sun* daily newspaper carries details of many of the events. Keep an eye also on flyers posted up around the island; local radio stations (see p.30) also advertise major events.

ANTIGUA TOURIST OFFICES OVERSEAS

Britain Antigua House, 15 Thayer St, London W1M 5LD, ☏ 020/7486 7073, fax 7486 9970.

ANTIGUA ON THE INTERNET

As you'd expect, the island has produced plenty of Web sites, covering everything from hotels, restaurants and tour groups to online daily newspapers and government departments. Below you'll find a few of the more helpful general sites on offer.

Antigua and Barbuda Tourist Authority
Ⓦ www.antigua-barbuda.org
The official site of the national tourism authority has info on forthcoming events as well as offers on places to stay and car rental outfits, many of which you can book with through the site.

Antigua Carnival Ⓦ www.antiguacarnival.com
The summer schedule is set out in detail, and there's a "scrapbook" of last year's carnival and details of this year's bands, some of whose songs you can download.

Antigua Nice Ⓦ www.antiguanice.com
Masses of information on the island, from hotel and restaurant reviews to details of travel agents and links to the island's latest news.

Cricket Ⓦ www.cricket.org
Given the importance of cricket you'd expect Antigua to have its own cricketing Web site, but for now the best way to find out information on matches is via this excellent, but generalized, site.

Nick Maley's Island Arts Ⓦ www.antiguatoday.com/IslandArts/
Online information from Nick Maley, creator of Yoda, about his Island Arts business (see p.53), and helpful links to other informative Antigua-based sites.

Sailing week Ⓦ www.sailingweek.com and
Ⓦ www.antiguaclassics.com
Both sites are packed with information on the two weeks in April when Antigua's sailing tradition really comes into its own.

Canada 60 St Clair Ave E, Suite
304, Toronto, ON M4T IN5,
☎ 416/961-3085, fax 961-
7218.
USA 610 5th Ave, Suite 311,
New York, NY 10020, ☎ 212/
541-4117, fax 757-1607;
25 SE 2nd Ave, Suite 300,
Miami, FL 33131, ☎ 305/381-
6762, fax 381-7908.
*(The ATO has no branches in
Australia or New Zealand)*

Money and costs

A ntigua is not a particularly cheap country to visit,
and prices for many items are at least as much as
you'd pay at home. Negotiation on price is generally
frowned on – taxi rates, for example, are normally fixed –
but, particularly during the off-season of April to
November, it can be worth asking for a reduced rate for
items such as accommodation or car rental.

CURRENCY

The island's unit of currency is the **Eastern Caribbean
dollar** (EC$), divided into 100 cents. It comes in bills of

MONEY AND COSTS

$100, $50, $20, $10 and $5 and coins of $1, $0.50, $0.25, $0.10, $0.05 and $0.01. The rate of exchange is fixed at EC$2.70 to US$1 (giving you, at the time of writing, roughly EC$4 to UK£1), though you'll get a fraction less when you exchange money. In tourist-related business, the US$ is often used as an unofficial parallel currency, and you'll often find prices for hotels, restaurants and car rental quoted in US$ (a policy we have adopted in this guide). Bear in mind, though, that you can always insist on paying in EC$ (and the exchange rate usually works out slightly in your favour). If you are using US dollars or travellers' cheques to pay a bill, check in advance whether your change will be given in the same currency (it usually won't).

COSTS

Apart from the flight, **accommodation** is likely to be the major expense of your trip, and most visitors pay this up front as part of a package. For those booking locally, double rooms start at around US$25, though most of the cheaper options cost around US$35–40 in winter, US$30–35 in summer. For something more salubrious, expect to pay at least US$70–80 in winter, US$50–60 in summer. Rooms apart, if you **travel** around on foot and by bus and get your **food** from supermarkets and the cheaper cafés, you could just about survive on a **daily budget** of around US$15 per day. Upgrading to one decent meal out, the occasional taxi ride and a bit of evening entertainment, expect to spend a more realistic US$30–35 per day; after that, the sky's the limit.

TRAVELLERS' CHEQUES AND PLASTIC

The safest method of carrying money abroad is in the form of **travellers' cheques** and, while sterling and other currencies are perfectly valid and accepted in the island's banks, US dollar travellers' cheques are the best ones to have. They are available for a small commission from most banks, and from branches of American Express and Thomas Cook; make sure you keep the purchase agreement and a record of cheque serial numbers safe and separate from the cheques themselves. Once in Antigua, they can be cashed at banks (you'll need your passport or other photo ID to validate them) for a small charge.

Major credit cards – American Express, Visa, MasterCard – are widely accepted, but don't necessarily expect the smaller hotels and restaurants to take them. You can also use the cards to get cash advances at most banks, though you'll pay both commission to the bank and hefty interest to your credit card company.

Banking hours are generally Mon–Thurs 8am–3pm, Friday 8am–5pm; branches of the Caribbean Commercial Bank are also open on Saturday from 9am–noon (see p.134 for locations). Many **hotels** will also exchange money, though if you're changing anything other than US$ the rate is usually a bit worse than the banks.

EMERGENCY CASH

If you **run out** of money, and can't get it out of an ATM machine, you can arrange a telegraphic transfer to most of the banks in Antigua from your home bank account or that of a friend or family member. Bear in mind that such a transfer will attract hefty commission at both ends, so treat this very much as a last resort.

Communications
and the media

Antigua's **postal service** is reasonably efficient. The GPO in St John's is open Mon–Fri 8.15am–noon and 1–4pm (5pm Fri) and has poste restante facilities for receiving mail. There are also branches at the airport, at the Woods Centre and at English Harbour, and you can buy stamps and send mail at many of the hotels. **Postal rates** are reasonable: to the UK, USA and Canada, air mail EC$0.90, postcards EC$0.45; to Australasia, air mail EC$1.20, postcards $0.60.

Calling within Antigua is simple – most hotels provide a **telephone** in each room. You'll also see **phone booths** all over the island, and these can be used for local and international calls. Most of the booths take phonecards only – they're available at hotels, post offices and some shops and supermarkets. For finding numbers, hotel rooms and phone booths often have a directory; failing that, call directory assistance on ☎411. To reach the operator dial ☎0.

INTERNATIONAL CALLS

PHONING ANTIGUA FROM ABROAD
Dial your international access code (see below)
+ 268 + seven-digit number
UK ☎001   USA ☎011   Canada ☎011
Australia ☎0011   New Zealand ☎00

PHONING ABROAD FROM ANTIGUA
Dial country code (see below)
+ area code minus first 0 + number
UK ☎011 44   USA ☎1   Canada ☎1
Australia ☎011 61   New Zealand ☎011 64

PRESS AND RADIO

As always, local newspapers and radio are a great way to find out what's on the nation's mind. The daily *Antigua Sun* is the best paper, concentrating on domestic news but with a decent section on news from the wider Caribbean and the rest of the world and, invariably, a big sports section. The main radio stations are the public service channel **ABS** (620 AM), and the commercial **Sun FM** (100.1 FM). They both carry news, sport, chat shows and music, mostly international hits with a sprinkling of local tunes.

Festivals, events and public holidays

The main events in Antigua are the summertime **Carnival** (see p.119), and the April Sailing Week, but there are various other events to distract you from the beach, including international **cricket**, **tennis** and **warri** (a board game) tournaments. The local and overseas tourist boards have full details of all the activities.

ANNUAL EVENTS	
Jan	Red Stripe Cricket Competition ☏ 462 9090
Feb	Valentine's Day Regatta, Jolly Harbour ☏ 461 6324
March–April	Test cricket ☏ 462 9090
April	Classic Regatta ☏ 460 1799
	Sailing Week ☏ 460 8872
May	Pro-Am Tennis Classic
	Curtain Bluff Hotel ☏ 462 8400
July/Aug	Carnival see p.119, ☏ 462 4707

continues overleaf

from previous page

Sept	Bridge Championship	☎ 462 1459
Oct	National Warri Championship	☎ 462 6317
Nov	Antiguan Craft Fair Harmony Hall	☎ 460 4120
Dec	Nicholson's Annual Charter – Yacht Show,	☎ 460 1530

PUBLIC HOLIDAYS

New Year's Day	Jan 1
Good Friday	Friday before Easter Sunday
Easter Monday	day after Easter Sunday
Labour Day	first Mon in May
Whit Monday	end of May
Caricom Day	early July
Carnival	first Mon and Tues in Aug
United Nations Day	first Mon in Oct
Independence Day	Nov 1
Christmas Day	Dec 25
Boxing Day	Dec 26

ANNUAL EVENTS

Shopping

I f you want to take home something authentically Antiguan, check out the stores and **craft stalls** around Redcliffe Quay and Heritage Quay in St John's (see p.42), or wait for the vendors to find you – those on the most popular beaches, particularly Dickenson Bay on the northwest coast, regularly set up stands selling clothing, carved wooden figurines and Haitian-style paintings of markets and other traditional scenes. There are also some good art stores and plenty of T-shirt and craft vendors at Nelson's Dockyard on the south coast, while the shopping complex at Jolly Harbour Marina on the west coast has more art shops, souvenir stores, clothing boutiques and a sizeable supermarket.

Other than that, you're largely restricted to the familiar **duty-free** options, with a massive array at Heritage Quay (see p.49). If you're after duty-free liquor, jewellery, clothes, cameras or perfume, you'll find all the shops you need there (Mon–Sat 9am–5pm and Sun when there's a cruise ship in port). Take your passport or air ticket as proof of visitor status.

The island's main shopping mall is the modern **Woods Centre**, just outside St John's, where you'll find the island's best-equipped supermarkets, pharmacies, bookshops, opticians and numerous other stores. For general food shopping, grocery stores are dotted around the island, while the market in St John's is the most colourful place to visit (see p.47), particularly on Saturday morning when it hums with life and stands are piled high with yams, mangos, paw-paws and other fruit and vegetables; there are fish and meat sections too.

Drugs, trouble and harassment

Compared to what you'll encounter in Jamaica or several other Caribbean islands, **harassment** in Antigua is extremely mild. The itinerant vendors who patrol some of the beaches are the main culprits – you'll occasionally be offered drugs or pressed to look at some uninspiring crafts – but on the whole police crackdowns have kept them at a distance. If you're not interested, just be firm in saying no thanks and they'll leave you alone.

Violent crime involving tourists is rare but not unheard of. After dark, it's advisable to steer clear of unlit or unpatrolled areas of the beach, and you'll probably want to avoid the rougher areas of St John's, though there's no reason why you'd want to visit them. **Drugs** present an increasing problem on the island, particularly a growing use of crack cocaine, which is leading to a rise in theft and burglary to finance the habit. Marijuana use is just as widespread – and equally illegal – often distributed on the beaches, particularly on the south coast, to likely-looking punters. If you want it, you can get it, but bear in mind that there are plenty of undercover police around, and the local press runs stories daily of tourists facing heavy fines for possession.

Emergency numbers

Police ☎ 462 0125 • Fire ☎ 462 0044 • Ambulance ☎ 462 0251

THE GUIDE

1	St John's and around	39
2	From Runaway Bay to Half Moon Bay	51
3	Falmouth and English Harbour	58
4	The West Coast	71
5	Barbuda and Redonda	77

St John's and around

With a population of around 30,000 – nearly half the island's total – bustling **St John's** is Antigua's capital and only city. No one could accuse it of being the prettiest city in the West Indies, but it does have a certain immediate charm and, in the centre, there are plenty of attractive old wooden and stone buildings – some of them superbly renovated, others in a perilous state of near-collapse – among the less appealing modern development. It'll only take you a couple of hours to see everything but, even if you're not staying in the capital, you'll probably want to come back for at least one evening to take advantage of some excellent **restaurants** and **bars**.

There's no beach to speak of in St John's, though a short ride away **Fort Bay** has a lovely stretch of sand, absolutely packed at weekends and on holidays, while nearby **Fort James** is one of the best-preserved colonial forts on the island. The fort overlooks (and once protected) the narrow channel of water that has taken trading ships into the city's harbour for over 300 years.

Getting there and getting around

As all of the main places of interest in St John's are close together, the easiest way to see the place is **on foot**. Driving in the city is straightforward if not particularly enjoyable; parking space is limited, the one-way traffic system a little tricky to deal with, and potholes and roadside rain gullies threaten damage to your car at every turn. There are **taxi** stands just west of the market at the southern end of town, beside the east bus station near the Antigua Recreation Ground, and at Heritage Quay.

If you're arriving in or leaving the city by **bus**, the east bus station serves the north of the island (Dickenson Bay, Cedar Grove and the airport) and the east (Pares and Willikies), while the west bus station, beside the market, serves the west (Five Islands) and south (Jolly Harbour, Old Road, Falmouth and English Harbour).

Information

The government's main **tourist office** (☎ 462 0480), at the western end of Nevis Street, has a perfunctory smattering of brochures on the island and a free road map. For more practical information about any big events on while you're in town, you'll need to rely on flyers, newspaper and radio ads and word of mouth.

Safety and harassment

On the whole St John's is an extremely safe city and, during the daytime at least, you'll be undisturbed wandering around. There are a few hustlers who zero in on obvious foreigners – asking you to buy something or begging for change – but they are rarely persistent or threatening. At night most of the city is unlit and there is a little more of a

ST JOHN'S AND AROUND

sense of menace, particularly around the very poor areas to the south (though you'll never have any reason to venture there). Stick to the centre, where you'll find the restaurants and bars, and you're highly unlikely to encounter any hassle.

For details of accommodation in St John's, see p.90;
for eating and drinking see p.105.

The city

The small centre of **St John's** is easily explored on foot, and you should certainly make your way to **Redcliffe Quay** – where the waterfront and its colonial buildings have been attractively restored – as well as the tiny **National Museum**, which offers a well-presented run-down on the country's history and culture. If you've got time, take a stroll through some of the old streets, and check out the city's twin-towered **cathedral** perched on top of Newgate Street. **Redcliffe Quay** and nearby **Heritage Quay** are the best places to eat, drink and shop for souvenirs, though you'll probably want to avoid them if the cruise-ships are in, when the steel drums come out to play "Feeling Hot, Hot, Hot" and the area almost disappears beneath a scrum of duty-free shoppers.

Some history

Although it is now by far Antigua's biggest town, St John's was not the first major settlement on the island, a distinction that went to Falmouth on the south coast (see p.59). The first reference to St John's was made in the 1660s, when the colonists decided to build a town that could take

THE CITY

41

full advantage of the excellent natural harbour. Though St John's suffered almost immediate **invasion** by the French, who sailed in and destroyed the fledgling town in 1668, it quickly grew into a prosperous city which, with its great location at the northeastern corner of the Caribbean – making it one of the first islands to be reached by ships sailing from Europe – became the area's leading business centre.

The city's major buildings were determined by colonial Antigua's two chief concerns – **trade** and **security**. Warehouses were erected by the quays to store sugar and molasses prior to export and barracoons were built to hold the imported slaves, while forts were built at strategic points around the harbour to deter further invasion. Natural disasters and disease were regular visitors: in particular, a yellow fever epidemic in 1793 wiped out many of the inhabitants, while a devastating fire in 1841 gutted most of the city's old buildings.

As the nineteenth century progressed, the declining fortunes of sugar (see p.144) meant that St John's began to lose much of its former lustre and – though still the capital city – it gradually became something of a provincial backwater. However, the tourist boom of the last few decades has prompted a concerted effort to spruce the place up and, with the quay area in particular now well-restored, it is still possible to catch a whiff of the city's glory days.

AROUND REDCLIFFE QUAY

Map 3, D4.

Spread over several acres by the waterside, **Redcliffe Quay** is probably the best place to start your tour of the city. Named in honour of the church of St Mary Redcliffe in the English port city of Bristol, this is one of the oldest parts of St John's, and incorporates many old warehouses –

now attractively restored as small boutiques, restaurants and bars – and a wooden boardwalk that runs alongside the water. There's not a huge amount to see, but it's a pleasant place to wander and soak up some of the city's history.

Many of the waterfront warehouses once held supplies for the British navy and local merchant ships that traded between Antigua and the mother country during the eighteenth century – barrels of sugar and rum, lumber for ship repairs, cotton and sheepskins. The area behind the quay around the western end of Nevis Street held a number of barracoons, compounds where slaves were held after they arrived on the island and before they were sent off to the plantations or shipped on to other Caribbean islands. The recently-restored house at **Coates Cottage** on Nevis Street (named by Scottish settlers in honour of the mountain Ben Nevis) is built on the site of one such barracoon and, when the owner is there, he is happy for you to wander through to the small walled courtyard where the slaves were held. The adjacent wooden building was once a **bargaining house**, where auctions were held and slaves sold off to local estate-owners.

Back at the front of the quay, a short stroll north takes you up to **Heritage Quay** at the foot of High Street. This modern concrete quay is given over to cruise-ship arrivals and dozens of duty-free shops designed to catch their tourist dollars, along with a few roadside stalls where local vendors flog T-shirts and distinctive Haitian art. Unless you're shopping or heading to the King's Casino (see p.119), there's no reason to stop except for a quick look at the **cenotaph** – a memorial to Antiguans who died during World War I – a **monument to V.C. Bird** – first prime minister of the independent country – and the **Westerby Memorial**, which commemorates a Moravian missionary dedicated to helping Antiguans in the decades after emancipation from slavery in 1834.

For more information on shopping opportunities here see p.49.

LONG STREET AND AROUND

From the water, Long Street runs east as far as the **Antigua Recreation Ground**, the country's main cricket venue and the home to most of the action during the ten-day Carnival each July and August (see p.119). The street has many of St John's finest old buildings, including a couple of fabulously colourful liquor stores, still in operation more than a century after first opening.

THE REC

Modest and unassuming as it looks, the Antigua Recreation Ground is one of the finest cricket pitches in the Caribbean. Blessed by low rainfall and year-round sun, and with its outfield and wicket lovingly tended by trusted inmates from the nearby prison, it looks at quiet times like any cricket pitch in England or Australia. Don't believe it for a moment. On match days, while the rest of the island comes to a standstill, the ground is transformed into a cacophonous whirligig, with music belting from the stands, hordes of vendors flogging jerk chicken and Red Stripe, men on stilts and women in wigs.

If you've got any sense of adventure, head for Chickie's Double Decker stand at the north end of the ground. With his banks of huge speakers tied to the railings, the eponymous deejay blasts players and fans alike with the songs of local Calypsonians, and everyone sings along to the chorus of "Rally round the West Indies". Bumping and grinding away, more intent on the beer and the chat-up lines than the cricket, the happy spectators will be there long after stumps have been drawn and the players have retired to the pavilion.

The National Museum

Map 3, E2. Mon–Fri 8.30am–4pm, Sat 10am–2pm; free.

Housed in a 1747 Neoclassical courthouse on the corner of Long and Market streets, the **National Museum of Antigua and Barbuda** occupies just one large room, but it's indisputably worth thirty minutes of your time while you're exploring the capital – you can almost feel the enthusiasm with which the collection has been assembled and displayed. The exhibits start by showing off the islands' early geological history, backed up by fossils and coral skeletons, and move on to more extensive coverage of its first, Amerindian inhabitants. Jewellery, primitive tools, pottery shards and religious figures used by these early settlers have been found at sites across Antigua and Barbuda and are well laid out, with brief descriptions of their significance.

Continuing chronologically, there are brief displays on Columbus, the European invasion and sugar production – the country's *raison d'être* from the mid-seventeenth century. An interesting 1750 map of Antigua shows the plantations, as well as all the reefs that threatened shipping around the island. There is also an unusual exhibit on the emancipation of the slaves and the resulting patterns of settlement. At emancipation in 1834 there were only four towns on Antigua, with almost all the ex-slaves living on the sugar estates; the planters usually refused to sell them land, since they wanted to keep them tied to the plantations. The exhibit shows how – with the assistance of missionaries or by sheer determination – the former slaves were able to set themselves up in "free villages" across the island.

For more on Antigua's early Amerindian population, see "A Brief History of Antigua", p.139.

LONG STREET AND AROUND

VIVI

One of the museum's most prized exhibits is the cricket bat with which, in 1986, Antiguan **Vivian Richards** (now Sir Vivian) scored the fastest-ever test-match century, taking just 56 balls to score 100 runs against England on his home turf. It's hard to overestimate the importance of Vivi (as he's known locally) to the development of the country's self-confidence in the years immediately before and after independence in 1981. For this tiny island to have produced a man rated by many as the finest batsman of his generation was an enormous boost to its self-esteem. Richards wasn't the first Antiguan to play for the West Indies cricket team – fast bowler Andy Roberts won that honour a few months earlier – but his spectacular hitting and imperious manner endeared him to a generation of cricket-watchers worldwide. Now retired, Richards has eschewed the political career many expected, but the street where he was born in St John's now bears his name and – as a "goodwill ambassador" – he remains one of Antigua's most precious living assets.

Elsewhere, there are displays on the island of Barbuda – which might whet your appetite for a visit (see p.77) – and the tiny uninhabited rock of Redonda (see p.86). There's also an example of the ancient board game warri or mancala, brought by slaves from Africa's Gold Coast, and, rather bizarrely, a rhinoceros skull from Rwanda. Once you've finished your tour, take a peek in the small **gift shop**, where you can pick up pottery, reproduction maps of the islands, postcards and books.

ST JOHN'S CATHEDRAL

Map 3, F2. Daily 9am–5pm; free.
East of here, and towering over the city at the far end of

Newgate Street, the imposing twin towers of the **Cathedral Church of St John the Divine** are the capital's dominant landmark. A simple wooden church was first built on this hilltop site in 1681 and, after heavy destruction was wrought by a number of earthquakes and hurricanes, the present cathedral was put up in 1847.

From the outside, the grey-stone Baroque building is not particularly prepossessing – squat and bulky with the two towers capped by slightly awkward cupolas. More attractively, the airy interior of the cathedral is almost entirely encased in dark pine, designed to hold the building together in the event of earthquake or hurricane, and the walls are dotted with marble tablets commemorating distinguished figures from the island's history, some of them rescued from the wreck of earlier churches here and incorporated into the new cathedral. In the grounds of the cathedral, the whitewashed and equally Baroque **lead figures** on the south gate – taken from a French ship near Martinique in the 1750s during the Seven Years War between France and Britain – represent St John the Baptist and St John the Divine, draped in flowing robes.

THE MARKET

Map 3, E6. Mon–Sat from around 6am.

One other colourful site worth checking out is the public **market** at the south end of Market Street, a road once known as Scotch Row in honour of the traders – many of them early Scottish immigrants who fled to the West Indies to escape the tyranny of seventeenth- and eighteenth-century English landowners – who once lined it with their shops selling sugar, indigo, coffee, tobacco and rum. Today it remains an important shopping thoroughfare, with the public market the place to head to for exotic fruit, vegetables and fish. As you'd expect, it's a lively, bustling place with a fine variety of food, particularly on Friday and Saturday – head down and pick up some sapodillas, papayas and mangoes for great snacking.

Fort Bay

A short drive or taxi-ride from town, heading north from St John's on Fort Road, a left turn at the old pink *Barrymore Hotel* (just north of the Texaco station) takes you out to the capital city's most popular beach and some of the best-preserved **military ruins** on the island. The road winds its way around to the coast at **Fort Bay**, where a long, wide strand of grainy white sand – packed with city dwellers at weekends and holidays – offers the nearest quality beach to town. At its northern end, you can hire beach chairs from *Millers* – a good place, too, to pick up a drink (see p.107) – and there's a vendors' mall nearby if you want to hunt for souvenirs.

At the other end of the strip, 500 metres further on, a host of food and drink stalls open up at busy times when a crowd descends from town, transforming the place into a lively outdoor venue, with music blaring, fish frying and plenty of frolicking on the beach. If you want to swim, there's a protected, marked area at the top of the beach; elsewhere, the water is normally fine but you'll need to watch out for occasional undercurrents.

FORT JAMES

Map 2, C3. Always open; free.

At the far end of Fort Bay stands eighteenth-century **Fort James**, built up above the cliffs that overlook the entrance to St John's harbour. You can walk or drive around to the south side of the fort, where the main gate is still in place. Together with Fort Barrington, on the opposite side of the channel (see p.76) and St John's Fort on Rat Island – still visible down the channel – this fort was designed to deter any ships from attacking the capital, which had been sacked by French raiders in 1668. Earthworks were first raised in the 1680s, though the bulk of the fort was put up in 1739, when the long enclosing wall was added. The place never fired a shot in anger, although its guns undoubtedly intimidated visiting vessels into paying the eighteen shillings levied in the eighteenth century to the fort's captain.

Today, the fort is pretty dilapidated but offers plenty of atmosphere: unkempt, often windswept and providing great views across the channel and back down to St John's harbour. Rusting British cannons from the early 1800s point out to sea and down the channel, their threat long gone but still a dramatic symbol of their era. Elsewhere, the old powder magazine is still intact, though leaning precariously, and the stone buildings on the fort's upper level – the oldest part of the structure, dating from 1705 – include the master gunner's house, the canteen and the barracks. At the northern tip of the fort, *Russell's* (see p.121) is a decent place to grab a drink and a snack after you've explored or head down to *Candyland* (see p.106) on the beach.

Shopping

St John's is a reasonable target for **shoppers** and, given its limited size, there's a surprising amount of choice. By the water, Heritage Quay has a broad range of **duty-free**

stores – including international chains like Body Shop and
Benetton – selling designer clothes, jewellery and liquor.
Non-chain stores like A Thousand Flowers and Sunseakers
offer a fine range of swimwear and casual outfits, while
Yoda-creator Nick Maley's Island Arts store has a selection
of paintings and prints by him (see p.53). Nearby Redcliffe
Quay has more designer clothes stores while, down a notch
in quality, the adjoining streets are crowded with stalls offering T-shirts, Haitian paintings and various **souvenir** knick-
knacks.

For **food**, there's the enormous Bryson's supermarket by
the quay at the bottom of Long Street (Mon–Sat 8am–9pm,
Sun 9am–4pm), and a range of tropical fruit, vegetables and
fish at the market downtown. There's not much else around
the city, although the beautiful old **liquor** stores on Long
Street stock Antigua's Cavalier and English Harbour rums as
well as other, better Caribbean rums, including Barbados's
Mount Gay Extra Old and Haiti's Barbancourt Reserve.

The American mall-style Woods Centre, a couple of
minutes' drive north of town, is mainly targeted at
Antiguan shoppers, and oozes local affluence. You'll find
the island's best-stocked **supermarket**, Epicurean (daily
8am–10pm), though prices are pretty hefty; its finest **book-
shop**, First Edition (Mon–Sat 9am–9pm); as well as banks,
fast-food outlets, a post office, a gym and plenty more. A
courtesy bus runs to the centre from the west bus station in
St John's, near the market. If you're on foot, follow Cross
Street north for 750 metres from its junction with Newgate
Street (see map 3).

From Runaway Bay to Half Moon Bay

Heading north of St John's, **Runaway Bay** and adjoining **Dickenson Bay** constitute the island's main tourist strip, with a couple of excellent beaches, a host of good hotels and restaurants and plenty of action. Continuing clockwise round the island brings you to its Atlantic side, where the jagged coastline offers plenty of inlets, bays and swamps but, with a couple of noteworthy exceptions, rather less-impressive beaches. Tourist facilities on this side of the island are much less developed, but there are several places of interest. **Betty's Hope** is a restored sugar plantation; **Parham**, the island's first port, has a lovely old church; **Devil's Bridge** offers one of the most dramatic landscapes on the island; at picturesque **Half Moon Bay** you can scramble along a vertiginous clifftop path above the pounding Atlantic; and at the delightful **Harmony Hall** you can relax from your exertions with an excellent lunch and a boat-ride to Green Island.

RUNAWAY BAY AND DICKENSON BAY

Map 4.

A few kilometres north of St John's, a series of attractive white-sand beaches run around the island's northwest coast. Most of the tourist development has happened along Runaway Bay and Dickenson Bay, where the gleaming beaches slope gently down into the turquoise sea, offering calm swimming and, at the northern end of Dickenson Bay, a host of watersports. **Runaway Bay** is the quieter of the two and, because there are fewer hotels to tidy up their "patch", is strewn with more seaweed and rocks. It's still a great place to wander in the gentle surf, though at the northern end much of the beach has been eroded by heavy swells.

Just beyond here, grassy **Corbison Point** pokes out into the sea, dividing the bay from Dickenson Bay. A stone igloo-shaped powder store is the sole remnant of an eighteenth-century British **fort** that once stood here, and the cliff has also revealed Amerindian potsherds and evidence that more ancient island-dwellers exploited flint in the area for their tools. Heading north of the point, you'll have to detour briefly onto the road to bypass the marina at the *Marina Bay Hotel*, before returning to the beach.

Trapped between two imposing sandstone bluffs, **Dickenson Bay** is fringed by another wide, white-sand beach, which stretches for almost a mile between Corbison Point and the more thickly vegetated woodland of Weatherill's Hill at its northern end. It's a lovely bay, shelving gently into the sea and with a protected swimming zone dividing swimmers from the jet-skiers, windsurfers, waterskiers and parasailers who frolic offshore. The northern half of the beach fronts some of the largest of Antigua's hotels, including the *Rex Halcyon Cove*, whose pier juts out into the sea and offers dining above the ocean, and *Sandals*

Antigua, with its striking yellow pavilions. As a result, particularly in high season, the area can get pretty busy, with a string of bars, hair-braiders and T-shirt sellers doing a brisk trade, but it's still an easy-going place, with minimal hassle.

Divided by the coast road from Runaway Bay and the southern end of Dickenson Bay, **McKinnon's Salt Pond** is an extensive area of brackish water edged by mangroves and a good place for bird-spotting. More than 25 species of water birds have been recorded here, most noticeably the big flocks of sandpipers wheeling above the pond, as well as terns and plovers that nest on the sand and redfooted herons that breed in the mangroves. Seabirds can also be seen at either end of the beach, swooping gracefully around the sandstone bluffs; watch out in particular for the pelicans, showing off their clumsy but spectacular technique of dive-bombing for fish.

For details of accommodation in Runaway Bay and Dickenson Bay, see p.92; for eating and drinking see p.109.

ISLAND ARTS

Map 2, E1. Mon–Fri 9am–5pm.

There are few points of interest worth stopping off for on the northeast coast, but Nick Maley's **Island Arts Gallery** in Hodges Bay is certainly one of them. Maley, originally a film make-up artist who worked on movies like *Star Wars* and *Krull*, is a British painter who has worked on Antigua for over a decade and shown his striking and original works at exhibitions across the Caribbean and North America. Maley's small gallery and studio – resonating to the squawks of the parrots he and his wife breed in their lush garden – are crammed with his paintings and prints, as well as those of Antiguan, Haitian and other West Indian artists. Though the artists are mostly little-known outside their home islands, there is plenty of exuberant colour and some captivating local portraits beside the more predictable land and seascapes. The gallery is signposted up a side street, off the main road that skirts the northeast coast. If you want to meet Maley, call ahead on ☎ 461 6324 as he's sometimes at his Heritage Quay store in St John's.

FITCHES CREEK BAY AND PARHAM

Map 2, E3 and F3.

East of the airport, a rocky road loops round **Fitches Creek Bay**, a desolate inlet with no beaches of note, dotted with brackish mangrove swamps; bird-watchers can look out for herons, egrets and whistling ducks among the multitude of local species. **St George's Parish Church**, first built in 1687 – though hurricane and earthquake damage have each long since taken their toll – overlooks the bay. Recent reconstruction of the place is largely complete, the church having been gutted and a new roof raised, but the ancient, weathered brick walls and crumbling tombs facing out to sea still lend it a strong sense of history.

The road continues around the bay to **PARHAM**. First settled in the seventeenth century, it is one of the oldest inhabited towns on the island. By far the most impressive building in town is the octagonal **St Peter's Parish Church**, considered unique in the Caribbean. A wooden church was first erected here in 1711, although the present structure mostly dates from 1840. The inside is spacious and airy, with tall windows capped with brick arches and a handful of marble commemorative tablets to nineteenth-century local notables. The unusual wooden ribbed ceiling is especially striking; the design – like an upturned ship's hull – has delightful simplicity.

Outside, the cemetery tumbles down the hill towards **Parham Harbour**, Antigua's first port. Protected from the Atlantic waves by offshore islands, this fine natural anchorage was busy with oceangoing ships for more than two centuries until sugar exports slumped in the 1920s. Now it shelters yachts and small fishing vessels – there's a small jetty at the eastern end of town but few other port facilities to testify to its heyday.

BETTY'S HOPE

Map 2, F4. Tues–Sat 10am–4pm; EC$5.

From Parham, the road leads south and then east at the petrol station towards the partly restored **Betty's Hope**, the island's very first sugar estate. Built in 1650, the place was owned by the Codrington family for nearly two centuries until the end of World War II; by that time its lack of profitability had brought it to the edge of closure, which followed soon after. Although most of the estate still lies in ruins, one of the windmills has been restored to working condition, and a small and interesting museum at the visitor centre tells the history of sugar on Antigua and explains the development and restoration of the estate.

DEVIL'S BRIDGE AND LONG BAY

Map 2, H4.

East of Betty's Hope, the landscape becomes more prairie-like, with cattle roaming over the gently rolling hills. On your left, the otherwise unremarkable **St Stephen's Anglican Church** has been rebuilt to a curious design, with the pulpit in the centre and the pews on each side; outside, the crumbling tombs in the flower-strewn cemetery suggest that the place has been a religious site for several centuries.

Approaching Long Bay, a track signposted off to the right takes you out for one kilometre to **Devil's Bridge**, on a rocky outcrop edged by patches of grassy land, tall century plants and sunbathing cattle. Wander round the promontory to the "bridge", a narrow piece of rock whose underside has been washed away by thousands of years of relentless surf action. The hot, windswept spot offers some of the most fetching views on the island, back across a quiet cove to the *Mango Bay Hotel* and out across the lashing ocean and dark reefs to a series of small islands just offshore. En route back to the main road, a dirt track on your right after 400 metres leads down to a tiny but gorgeous bay – the perfect venue for a picnic. The place plays occasional host to some local parties, and can get rather litter-strewn, but the turquoise sea is exceptionally inviting and the normally empty strip of white beach a great place to chill out.

Past the turn-off for Devil's Bridge, at the end of the main road, **Long Bay** is home to a couple of rather exclusive all-inclusives, which doesn't stop you from getting access to a great, wide bay, enormously popular with local schoolkids, who can often be found splashing around or playing cricket at one end of the beach. The lengthy spread of white sand is protected by an extensive reef a few hundred metres offshore – bring your snorkelling gear – and there's a great little beach bar for shelter and refreshment when you've had enough sun.

HARMONY HALL AND GREEN ISLAND

Map 2, G5 and H4. Closed May to Oct.

Tucked away on the east coast overlooking Nonsuch Bay, the restored plantation house at **Harmony Hall** is now home to a tiny, chic hotel and one of the island's best restaurants as well as an art gallery that showcases monthly exhibitions of local and Caribbean art from November to

April. Though it's well away from the main tourist hang-outs and a little awkward to reach (down some poor-quality roads), it's a relaxed, friendly and delightful place. From the jetty, boats regularly make the five-minute run out to deserted **Green Island**, where the beaches are powdery and the snorkelling excellent. If you're not a guest, there's a small charge for the boat service – ask at the bar.

HALF MOON BAY

Map 2, H5.

One of the prettiest spots on Antigua, **Half Moon Bay** has a kilometre-long semicircle of white-sand beach partially enclosing a deep-blue bay, where the Atlantic surf normally offers top-class body-surfing opportunities. The isolation of this side of the island means that the beach is often pretty empty, especially since the 1995 closure, after Hurricane Luis, of the expensive hotel at its southern end. However, there is a car park beside the beach and a shack selling drinks and snacks.

THE HIKE ALONG SOLDIER POINT

There's an excellent 45-minute circular hike around Soldier Point, the headland at the southern end of Half Moon Bay, just beyond the hotel. Where the beach ends you can clamber up onto the rocks and a trail – marked by splashes of blue paint along its entire length – cuts left along the edge of the cliff. It's a moderately tough climb, with a bit of a scramble required in places, but well worth it for some fine views out to sea and over the bay, dramatic scenery carved by the waves and – apart from butterflies and seabirds – a sense of splendid isolation. Don't go barefoot – the rocks are sharp in places and there are plenty of thorns around.

Falmouth and English Harbour

An essential stop on any visit to Antigua, the picturesque area around **Falmouth** and **English Harbour** on the island's south coast holds some of the most important and interesting historical remains in the Caribbean and is now the region's leading yachting centre. The chief attraction is the eighteenth-century **Nelson's Dockyard**, which was the key facility for the British navy that once ruled the waves in the area. Today it's a living museum where visiting yachts are still cleaned, supplied and chartered, with several ruined forts nearby as well as an abundance of attractive colonial buildings on the waterfront, several now converted into hotels and restaurants.

Across the harbour from the dockyard, there is further evidence of the colonial past at **Shirley Heights**, where more ruined forts, gun batteries and an old cemetery hold a commanding position over the water. It's a dramatic place whose rather forlorn air is shattered on Sunday evenings when steel and reggae bands lend sound to a lively (if somewhat over-touristed) barbecue party.

For details of accommodation in Falmouth and English Harbour, see p.97; for eating and drinking see p.112

The area also has a handful of far-less-visited spots that repay a trip, including the massive military complex at **Great Fort George**, high in the hills above **Falmouth**, and the wonderful **Rendezvous Bay** – outstanding in an area with a paucity of good beaches – a short boat ride or less than an hour's hike from Falmouth.

Getting there and getting around

A car is invaluable for touring around this area of the south coast. There are frequent **buses** between St John's and English Harbour, handy if you just want to explore Nelson's Dockyard, but to get up to Shirley Heights you'll certainly need your own transport or a taxi.

Falmouth and around

The main road south from St John's, cutting through the very centre of Antigua, first hits the coast at **Falmouth Harbour**. This large and beautiful natural harbour has been used as a safe anchorage since the days of the earliest colonists, and the town that sprang up beside it was the first major settlement on the island. Today, though the harbour is still often busy with yachts, Falmouth itself is a quiet place, most of the activity in the area having moved east to **English Harbour** and Nelson's Dockyard, divided from Falmouth Harbour by a small peninsula known as the Middle Ground.

THE HIKE TO RENDEZVOUS BAY

Although there is no beach of particular note in Falmouth, you can make a great **hike** from just west of town to Rendezvous Bay, the most idyllic and one of the quietest beaches on Antigua. Heading out of town, turn left on Farrell Avenue and follow the road round past the colourful Rainbow School onto a dirt track edged with banana groves. Take a right at the first intersection, past the Spring Hill Riding Club, then, at the fork, go left up a hill that soon becomes paved. There's a big, white house at the top of the hill; park near it and follow the track that veers off to the left. If you don't have a car, it'll take you around 25 minutes to reach this point from the top of Farrell Avenue.

The track climbs briefly between Cherry Hill and Sugar Loaf Hill, allowing great views back over Falmouth Harbour, then drops down through the scrubby bush, with sea grape and acacia trees on either side. After 25 minutes you'll reach a rocky bay, strewn with conch shells, and a further ten-minute wander along the beach brings you to Rendezvous Bay, an aquamarine sea with a curve of fine white sand backed by coconut palms and dotted with driftwood. It's a gorgeous place to swim – the comparatively remote location means that there is rarely anyone else here, although the occasional boat trip makes its way across from Falmouth to use a thatched barbecue hut on the beach which offers welcome shade. Bring some water, a picnic, a book and some snorkelling gear, and you could easily spend half a day here.

There's little in town to stop for, but you may want to pay a brief visit to **St Paul's Church**, right alongside the main road. The original wooden church (long since destroyed by a hurricane) was the island's first, dating from the 1660s. Its modern successor is rarely open, but among the cracked eighteenth-century tombstones that cover the east side of the extensive graveyard is that of James Pitt, brother of the British Prime Minister, who died in English Harbour in 1780.

GREAT FORT GEORGE

Map 5, C1.

High above Falmouth, and offering terrific panoramic views over the harbour and surrounding countryside, are the ruins of **Great Fort George** (also known as **Monk's Hill**), one of Antigua's oldest defences. During the late seventeenth century, England was at war with France, whose navy captured the nearby island of St Kitts in 1686. To repel any invaders, the English decided to build a large fort on the hills behind the island's main town, together with housing and water cisterns to provide a secure retreat for Antigua's tiny population.

Though the French never in fact invaded, the fort was eventually completed in 1705, with dozens of cannon pointing in all directions. Barracks and gunpowder stores were added during the following century. With its seemingly impregnable position, Great George is likely to have been an important factor in deterring possible invasion. By the mid-nineteenth century, when any threat of invasion had receded, the fort was employed as a signal station, using flags to report on the movement of ships in and around Falmouth harbour.

For more on the colonial history of Antigua, see p.139.

Today, the fort is in a very ruinous state, but it's well worth the effort to get to for the fabulous views and – as there's rarely anyone there – a quiet but evocative sense of the island's past. Much of the enormous stone perimeter wall is intact while, inside the main gate and to the right, the west gunpowder magazine (built in 1731) has been well

GREAT FORT GEORGE

restored. It's fun to wander around the rest of the extensive scrub-covered ruins and see if you can identify which part was living quarters and which part military establishment.

To get to the fort you'll need a four-wheel-drive vehicle or a thirty-minute hike. A precipitous but passable track leads up from the village of Cobbs Cross, east of Falmouth; alternatively, from Liberta (north of Falmouth) take the inland road to Table Hill Gordon, from where another track winds up to the fort.

English Harbour and around

The road east from Falmouth leads to the tiny village of Cobb's Cross, where a right turn takes you down to the small village of **ENGLISH HARBOUR**, which today consists of little more than a handful of homes, shops and restaurants. Another right turn leads down to **Nelson's Dockyard**, to the excellent **Pigeon Beach** and to the Middle Ground peninsula that divides Falmouth Harbour from English Harbour. Alternatively, head straight on for the road that climbs up into the hills to the military ruins at **Shirley Heights**.

NELSON'S DOCKYARD

Map 5, E5. Daily 8am–6pm; EC$13 (also gets entry to Shirley Heights).

One of Antigua's definite highlights, the eighteenth-century **Nelson's Dockyard** is the only surviving Georgian dockyard in the world, and a delightful place to wander in.

"THIS INFERNAL HOLE"

The link between British Admiral **Horatio Nelson** and the dockyard named in his honour is somewhat tenuous. From 1784 to 1787, Nelson (aged 26 at the start of his tour of duty) commanded the Northern Division of the Leeward Island Station, based in English Harbour. There is little suggestion that he enjoyed his posting, indeed he referred to Antigua in correspondence as "a vile spot" and "this infernal hole". No doubt he was itching to engage the French in battle – something that he was to achieve (to his cost) some twenty years later – rather than sitting around swatting mosquitoes and chasing pirates. Nonetheless, after restoration in the 1950s the Antigua tourist board evidently decided a famous title was needed to help market the place, and so the name Nelson's Dockyard was born.

Adjacent to a fine natural harbour, the place developed primarily as a careening station – a place where British ships were brought to have the barnacles scraped from their bottoms and generally put back into shape. It provided a crucial function for the military, providing them with a local base to repair, water and supply the navy that patrolled the West Indies and protected Britain's prized colonies against enemy incursion.

The dockyard was begun in 1743, and most of the present buildings date from between 1785 and 1792, many of them – like the atmospheric *Admiral's Inn* hotel – built from the ballast of bricks and stones brought to the island by British trading ships, who sailed "empty" from home en route to loading up with sugar and rum.

During the nineteenth century, however, the advent of steam-powered ships, which needed less attention, coincided with a decline in British interest in the region, and the dockyard fell into disuse, finally closing in 1889. Over

NELSON'S DOCKYARD

the next sixty years the buildings took a battering from hurricanes and earthquakes, but the 1950s saw a major restoration project, and in 1961 the dockyard was officially reopened as both a working harbour and a tourist attraction.

The sights

The main road from English Harbour ends at a parking area, from where the entrance to the dockyard – where you can pick up an information sheet on the area – takes you past the local post office, a bank and a small **covered market**, where vendors compete languidly for custom for their T-shirts and other local souvenirs.

Entering the lane beyond this mini-commercial zone, the first building on your left is the **Admiral's Inn**, built in 1788 and originally used as a store for pitch, lead and turpentine, with offices for the dockyard's engineers upstairs. Today the place acts as a hotel and restaurant, and is one of the most atmospheric spots on the south coast. Adjoining the hotel, a dozen thick, capped **stone pillars** – looking like the relics of an ancient Greek temple – are all that remain of a large boathouse, where ships were pulled in along a narrow channel to have their sails repaired in the sail-loft on the upper floor.

From the hotel, a lane leads down to the harbour, passing various restored colonial buildings, including the remains of a guardhouse, a blacksmith's workshop and an old canvas and clothing store that provided supplies for the ships. On your right is a 200-year-old sandbox tree and, just beyond it, the Admiral's House (a local residence that never actually housed an admiral) which was built in 1855 and today serves as the dockyard's **museum**. The museum (daily 8am–6pm; free) is worth a quick tour for its small but diverse collection that focuses on the dockyard's history and on the island's shipping tradition, with models and

WALKING ON THE MIDDLE GROUND

For some rather more strenuous hiking, a right turn just before you reach Fort Berkeley leads up a poorly-defined track to the peninsula known as the Middle Ground, where more military ruins dot the landscape. It's a stiff clamber to the top of the hill, where a circular base is all that remains of the one-gun Keane battery that stood here until the early nineteenth-century, but you get a clear picture of the strategic importance of the Middle Ground for defending both Falmouth Harbour to the west and English Harbour to the east.

Continuing the hike on the other side of the hill leads down and then up to the remains of Fort Cuyler, where more gun emplacements and crumbling barracks walls are further testimony to the military domination of the area. You'll need all your tracking skills to keep to the paths around here – goats and the occasional goatherd are the only users of the old soldiers' tracks these days, and there is a fair amount of prickly cactus and thorn bush to contend with – but the hike offers spectacular views over the harbours and the ocean, as well as the desert-like landscape.

photographs of old schooners and battleships. Also look out for the cups and records celebrating the various races held during the annual Sailing Week, when English Harbour almost disappears under a tide of visiting yachts, their owners and crews.

For more information on Sailing Week at
English Harbour, see p.129.

Just beyond the museum, the bougainvillea-festooned **Copper and Lumber Store** now serves as an elegant hotel and restaurant; beyond that are the officers' quarters – one of the most striking buildings in the dockyard, with a

NELSON'S DOCKYARD

graceful double-staircase sweeping up to a long, arcaded veranda. Ships' officers lived here during the hurricane season, when most of the fleet put into English Harbour for protection. The building sits on a huge water cistern of 12 separate tanks, with a capacity for 240,000 gallons of water, and today provides space for an art gallery, boutique, bar and other stores, while the downstairs offices house the immigration and customs authorities.

Across from the building, several black-and-white **capstans** – formerly enclosed in a capstan house – have been thoroughly restored. These were used in the careening of ships; each mast was roped to a capstan, which was then rotated to turn the ship on its side. Behind the capstan and surrounded by iron railings is an old sundial.

FORT BERKELEY

Map 5, F6.

The narrow path that leads from behind the copper and lumber store to **Fort Berkeley** is easily overlooked, but a stroll around these dramatic military ruins should be an integral part of your visit. Built onto a narrow spit of land that commands the entrance to English Harbour, the fort was the harbour's earliest defensive point and retains essentially the same shape today that it had in 1745.

The path leads down to the water's edge; go around the jetty and some steps take you up to a trail leading to the fort, ten-minutes' walk away out on to the headland. On your right as you approach, above the craggy wave-swept rocks, cannons once lined most of the wall facing out to sea, with the main body of the fort at the far end of the walkway comprising sentry boxes, a recently restored guardhouse and a gunpowder magazine or store. A handful of early nineteenth-century Scottish cannons are still dotted around the ruined fort, and the place offers spectacular views out to sea and back across the sand-fringed harbour.

In 1750, to deter surprise attacks by small boats, a chain was stretched across the mouth of the harbour between Fort Berkeley and its sister fort, Fort Charlotte. Today, the chain is long gone and little more than rubble remains of Charlotte, destroyed by the same 1843 earthquake that demolished much of the original wall of Fort Berkeley.

PIGEON BEACH

Map 5, C4 and C5.

There's not much in the way of beach around Nelson's Dockyard but a good place to head for sand after some sightseeing is **Pigeon Beach**, five-minutes drive or twenty-minutes walk, west of the dockyard. As you head out, turn left just before the harbour and follow the road past a series of restaurants and the Antigua yacht club. Keep going past the *Falmouth Harbour Apartments*, take the uphill track that goes sharply left and follow the road down to the right, where you'll find a wide expanse of white sand and a welcoming **beach bar** (though the bar is sometimes closed during the summer).

SHIRLEY HEIGHTS

Map 5, G6. Open daily; from 9am–5pm there's a EC$13 entry charge which also gets entry to Nelson's Dockyard.

Spread over an extensive area of the hills to the east of English Harbour, numerous ruined military buildings offer further evidence of the strategic importance of this part of southern Antigua. Collectively known as **Shirley Heights** (although technically this is only the name for the area around Fort Shirley), it's an interesting area to explore, with a couple of hiking opportunities for the adventurous who want to escape the crowds completely.

Some history

The area of Shirley Heights is named after General Sir Thomas Shirley, governor of the Leeward Islands based in Antigua from 1781 to 1791. At a time when British Caribbean possessions were fast falling to the French – Dominica in 1778, St Vincent and Grenada in 1779 – and with British forces in America surrendering in 1781, Shirley insisted on massive fortification of Antigua to protect the naval dockyard. Building continued steadily for the next decade and, although the threat diminished after the French were finally defeated in 1815, the military complex was manned until 1854, since when it has been steadily eroded by a succession of hurricanes and earthquakes.

The sights

Follow the road uphill from the tiny village of English Harbour and you'll pass the late eighteenth-century **Clarence House**, an attractive Georgian house built in 1787 for Prince William, Duke of Clarence (later King William IV) who was then serving in the Royal Navy. At the time of writing, the house is under renovation. Past here, a right hand turn-off leads down to the *Inn at English Harbour* and the attractive crescent of Galleon Beach, where numerous yachts are normally moored at anchor just off-shore.

Ignoring the turn-offs and carrying straight on you'll pass the **Dow Hill Interpretation Centre** (no separate cost) which, frankly, has virtually nothing to do with the history of the area and is pretty missable. Outside you'll find the scant remains of the **Dow's Hill fort**; indoors, there's a great collection of local shells and a fifteen-minute "multi-media" exhibition, with an adult voice answering a child's questions about the country's history from the Stone Age to the present.

Beyond the centre, the road runs along the top of a ridge before dividing where a large cannon has been upended in the centre of the road. Fork left for the cliff known as **Cape Shirley**, where you'll find a collection of ruined stone buildings – including barracks, officers' quarters and an arms storeroom – known collectively as the **Blockhouse**. On the eastern side a wide gun platform looks downhill to **Indian Creek** (see box overleaf), beyond that to the **Standfast Point** peninsula and Eric Clapton's enormous house and gatehouse, and beyond that over the vast sweep of Willoughby Bay. Every year, stories leak out of Clapton and friends like Elton John and Keith Richard turning up for a jam at one of the island's nightclubs.

If you take the right-hand fork at the half-buried cannon, the road will lead you up to the further ruins of Fort Shirley. On the right as you approach are the still grandly arcaded though now roofless officers' quarters, overgrown with grass and grazed by the ubiquitous goats; opposite, across a bare patch of ground, are the ruins of the military hospital and, in a small valley just below the surgeon's quarters, the **military cemetery** with its barely legible tombstones dating mostly from the 1850s and reflecting the prevalence of disease – particularly yellow fever – and an obelisk commemorating the men of the Dorset regiment who died in service during the 1840s.

The road ends at the fort itself, where a restored guardhouse now serves as an excellent little bar and restaurant. Beyond the guardhouse, the courtyard of the **Lookout** – where once a battery of cannons pointed out across the sea – now sees a battery of cameras snapping up the fabulous views over English Harbour, particularly on Sundays when the tourists descend in droves for the reggae and steel bands.

- -
For more information on live music at the Lookout, see p.122.
- -

SHIRLEY HEIGHTS

A HIKE TO INDIAN CREEK

From the blockhouse it's a short but steep downhill hike down to the bluff which overlooks Indian Creek where, scattered along the shoreline, some of the island's most important Amerindian finds have been made. The hike passes down through scrubby grassland tended by goats and strewn with cacti, including the rather phallic red and green Turk's head cacti. At the bottom of the hill there's a small, sheltered but rocky beach, not great for swimming, while the path continues up through a wood of cracked acacia trees and onto the deserted bluff, which offers grand views over the creek and, further east, over Mamora Bay and Willoughby Bay.

AROUND MAMORA BAY

Map 2, F6.

From Cobbs Cross, avoiding the right turn to English Harbour, the road runs east towards a couple of quiet bays, including tiny Mamora Bay and the huge curve of Willoughby Bay. It's an attractive drive, though there is little specific to see; Mamora Bay is now dominated by the exclusive *St James Club* and the road past Willoughby Bay winds up through pineapple fields towards the old Betty's Hope sugar plantation (see p.55) and the island's east coast.

The West Coast

Tourism makes a firm impression on Antigua's **west coast**, with hotels dotted at regular intervals between the little fishing village of **Old Road** in the south and the capital, St John's. Two features dominate the area: a series of lovely beaches, with **Darkwood** probably the pick of the bunch for swimming, snorkelling and beachcombing, and a glowering range of hills known as the **Shekerley Mountains** in the southwest, offering the chance for a climb and some panoramic views. The lush and thickly wooded **Fig Tree Hill** on the edge of the range is as scenic a spot as you'll find, and you can take a variety of **hikes** inland to see a side of Antigua overlooked by the vast majority of tourists. Due west of St John's, the **Five Islands** peninsula holds several hotels, some good beaches and the substantial ruins of the eighteenth-century **Fort Barrington**.

For details of accommodation on Antigua's west coast, see p.99; for eating and drinking see p.114.

LIBERTA AND SWETES

Map 2, E5.

Heading west from Falmouth, the first main village that you

run into is **LIBERTA**, the first "free village" established for emancipated slaves after the abolition of slavery in 1834. It's still one of the largest settlements on the island, though you'll find little reason to stop off and explore. Beyond Liberta, **SWETES** is best known as the birthplace of cricketer Curtley Ambrose, the West Indies' leading fast bowler during the 1990s, and of present-day local cricketing hero Ridley Jacobs.

For more on the Antiguan passion for cricket, see p.147.

FIG TREE HILL

Map 2, D6.

Heading west at Swetes, you can follow the main road through the most densely forested part of the island, **Fig Tree Hill**. You won't actually see any fig trees – the road is lined with bananas (known locally as figs) and mango trees as it carves its way through some gorgeous scenery down to the south coast at Old Road. About halfway along the drive, you can stop at a small roadside shack which calls itself the **Cultural Centre**, where you can get a drink and some fruit picked straight off the trees from local farms.

A track leads south from the shack to a **Reservoir** – the island's first – where you'll find picnic tables set up around the edge of the water. More serious hikers can take the **Rendezvous Trail**, which crosses the **Wallings Woodlands** to the nearly always empty beach a two-hour walk away at Rendezvous Bay (see p.60). Even a short stroll repays the effort; the woodlands are the best remaining example of the evergreen secondary forest that covered the island before the British settlers arrived, with more than thirty species of shrubs and trees, including giant mahogany trees, and masses of noisy birdlife. The trail starts on your left just before you reach the steps of the reservoir – bear in mind that, though it's pretty hard to get lost, the main path is little used and in places can quickly become overgrown and hard to make out.

There's another hike to the fabulous Rendezvous Bay from Falmouth on the south coast – see p.60.

OLD ROAD

Map 2, D6.

Once an important port and town, **OLD ROAD** derived its name from nearby Carlisle Bay – a safe anchorage or "road" for the early settlers – but was soon surpassed by the new "roads" of St John's and Falmouth Harbour. Today Old Road is a small and rather impoverished fishing village, enlivened by the swanky *Curtain Bluff* resort that hangs dramatically above the sea – and a superb swath of beach – on the eponymous sandstone bluff. Many local people have recently become passionate supporters of English football club Liverpool and its star striker Emile Heskey; his father was born and lived in the village before moving to England in the 1960s.

BOGGY PEAK

Map 2, C5.

Heading west from Old Road, the road follows the coast past a series of banana groves and pineapple plantations and around **Cades Bay**, offering delightful views out to sea over Cades Reef. On the right, a kilometre from Old Road, a track leads up into the Shekerley Mountains to **Boggy Peak**, at 400 metres, the highest point on the island. The panoramic view from the top – in good visibility you can even make out St Kitts, Guadeloupe and Montserrat – is well worth the steep drive or the one-hour climb. Unfortunately, the peak is now occupied by a communication station, safely tucked away behind a high-security fence, so you'll need to make arrangements to visit with Cable & Wireless in St John's (☎462 0840). If you haven't the time or the inclination, the views from outside the perimeter fence are almost as good.

DARKWOOD BEACH AND AROUND

Map 2, B5.

Continuing west through the village of **Urlings**, the road runs alongside a number of excellent beaches. First up is **Turner's Beach** and Johnson's Point, where the sand shelves down to the sea beside a couple of good beach bars, including *Turner's* (see p.116) where you can rent snorkelling gear. The snorkelling is better just north of here at **Darkwood Beach**, a great spot to stop and take a swim, with a wide stretch of beach running right alongside the main road. Look out for small underwater canyons just off-shore, and schools of squid and colourful reef fish. Beachcombers will find this one of the best places on the island to look for shells and driftwood. There are a couple of groves of casuarina trees for shade, and another friendly little beach bar that offers inexpensive local food. Last, **Coco Beach** is reached via a turn-off signposted to the *Cocobay Hotel* (see p.99); follow the track for 500 metres past some old sugar mills for another magnificent beach, again strewn with driftwood and edged by a turquoise sea.

Jolly Harbour

Covering an immense area (much of it reclaimed swampland and saltponds) north of Coco Beach, the 450-bedroom all-inclusive *Jolly Beach Resort* (see p.100) sprawls alongside a mile of one of Antigua's best beaches, with clear blue water lapping against the sugary white sand. Day-passes are available from the resort for around US$50 per day, including lunch, drinks and use of the watersports. Adjacent, the **Jolly Harbour** complex has a marina, rental apartments, a golf course, restaurants and a small shopping mall. It's a world apart from the "real" Antigua – like a small piece of America transplanted in the Caribbean.

GREEN CASTLE HILL

Map 2, D4.

If you haven't climbed Boggy Peak (see p.73) or Monk's Hill (see p.61), you could consider getting your panoramic view of Antigua from the top of **Green Castle Hill**. The peak is littered with natural formations of stone pillars and large rocks, claimed periodically as Stone Age megaliths left by Antigua's oldest inhabitants. The claim is patently absurd – there is no evidence of Antigua's Amerindians having either the technology or the inclination to erect such monuments to their deities – but don't let that put you off visiting. The views are superb, particularly to the north beyond St John's and, the odd goat aside, you won't see a soul around.

You'll really need a car to get there. Head inland from the main road between Jennings and St John's towards Emanuel; the path to the top (a forty-minute walk) begins by the gates of a small brick factory connected to a large stone quarry.

FIVE ISLANDS

Map 2, C3.

To the west of St John's the highway leads out through a narrow isthmus onto the large **Five Islands** peninsula, named after five small rocks that jut from the sea just offshore. There are several hotels on the peninsula's northern coast, a few more on its west coast, though the interior is largely barren and scrubby, and there's not a huge amount to see. A kilometre offshore from **Hawksbill Bay**, a large rock in the shape of the head of a hawksbill turtle gives the place its name. To reach the bay, and some more excellent beaches, follow the main road straight through the peninsula, ignoring the turn-offs for the *Yepton Hotel* and *Chez Pascal*.

On Goat Hill, at the northern point of the peninsula close to the *Royal Antiguan* hotel, the circular stone ruins of **Fort Barrington** overlook the gorgeous Deep Bay. The British first built a simple fort here in the 1650s, to protect the southern entrance to St John's Harbour, though it was captured by the French when they took the city in 1666. In 1779, at a time of renewed tension between the two nations, Admiral Barrington of the British navy enlarged and strengthened the fort. This time, the deterrent proved effective; like most of Antigua's defences, Fort Barrington never saw any further action, and spent the next two centuries as a signal station reporting on the movement of ships in the local waters. It's well worth the twenty-minute walk around the beach to the fort for the dramatic sense of isolation as you look out to sea or back over the tourists sunning themselves far below on the bay.

Barbuda and Redonda

With its magnificent and often deserted beaches, its spectacular coral reefs and its rare colony of frigate birds, the nation's other inhabited island, **Barbuda** – 48km to the north of Antigua – is well worth a visit. Don't expect the same facilities as on Antigua; **accommodation** options are limited, you'll need to bring your own snorkelling or diving gear, and you'll find that schedules – whether for taxis, boats or meals – tend to drift. This is all, of course, very much part of the island's attraction.

Barbuda is a throbbing metropolis, however, compared with Antigua's other "dependency", the tiny and now uninhabited volcanic rock known as **Redonda**, some 56km to the southwest in the main chain of the Lesser Antilles, between Nevis and Guadeloupe.

Barbuda

Half the size of its better-known neighbour, **Barbuda**

developed quite separately from Antigua and was only reluctantly coerced into joining the nation during the run-up to independence in 1981. The island is very much the "poor neighbour" in terms of financial resources, and its development has been slow; tourism has made only a minor impact, and fishing and farming remain the principal occupations of the tiny population of 1500, most of whom live in the small capital, **Codrington**.

The island is edged with powdery white-sand **beaches**, fringing an impossibly turquoise sea laced with coral reefs, perfect for snorkelling, diving and fishing. Along almost the entire length of the island's west coast run the mangrove swamps of **Codrington Lagoon**, home to the fabulous frigate birds. The **interior** is less fetching, mostly low-level scrub of cacti, bush, small trees and the distinctive century plants; for most of the year it is extremely arid and unwelcoming. There are a couple of exceptions: in the **southwest** the island suddenly bursts to life, with a fabulous grove of coconut palms springing out of the sandy soil (and providing a useful source of export revenue), while in parts of the **interior** government projects are reclaiming land from the bush to grow peanuts and sweet potatoes, also for the export market. For the most part, though, the island is left to the scrub, the elusive wild boar and deer and a multitude of birds – 170 species at last count.

Some history

Barbuda was first settled by a handful of English colonists in the 1620s, but the poor soil of this "barren rock", combined with attacks from Carib Indians from nearby islands, soon drove them off. Instead, livestock was released onto the island and periodically collected to feed the settlers on Antigua, St Kitts and Montserrat. In 1685 the English leased the island to the Codrington family, who were to hold it as private property for nearly 200 years. They

SHIPWRECKS

The shallows around Barbuda are littered with shipwrecks, the last resting place of some 150 vessels that failed to navigate safely through its dangerous coral reefs. Salvage from the wrecks was an important income for the islanders from at least 1695, when the *Santiago de Cullerin* ran aground with 13,000 pesos, destined for paying the garrisons on the Spanish Main in South America. During the following century ships hitting the reefs included slavers, cargo ships and warships, with the Barbudans recovering everything from cases of brandy to dried codfish, sugar and coal. Income from salvage reached a peak of around £7000 a year by the early 1800s, though improved navigation techniques during the following century saw the number of wrecks decline sharply.

continued to raise livestock for supplying both their sugar estates in Antigua and the Royal Navy at English Harbour.

None of the Codringtons ever lived on Barbuda, leaving management to a local "governor", who supervised a slave population that reached 500 at its peak. However, defences were erected, including a castle and a Martello tower, and a large house was built on the "Highlands", the ruins still evident today. Unlike Antigua, where slaves led a miserable existence chained to the sugar plantations, those in Barbuda had a relatively independent lifestyle, working as herdsmen, hunters, fishermen and shepherds. In the 1820s, an admittedly partisan Codrington wrote that his Barbuda slaves were "more happy, better fed and clothed and better off than the generality of peasants in England".

After emancipation of the slaves in 1834, the island remained privately owned until 1903, when it was adopted by the British Crown and administered alongside Antigua. In the run-up to independence in 1981, Barbudans made it clear that they wanted to remain independent of Antigua.

BARBUDA

Unfortunately for them, Britain sided with Antigua, and Barbuda took on its present status as a semi-autonomous dependency of its sister island, with its own elected council and a representative in the Antiguan parliament.

Getting there and getting around

The only scheduled **flights** to Barbuda are from Antigua on Carib Aviation (☎462 3147 or 462 3452, UK ☎01895 /450710, US ☎646/336-7600). They offer four flights a day from the main airport in Antigua (presently leaving at 7am, 8am, 9am and 5pm, returning thirty minutes later in each case) and charge US$50 round-trip. The planes take twenty minutes. More excitingly, the journey can be made by **boat**, although the cost of the 4hr crossing from St John's to River Landing on Barbuda's south coast tends to be pretty exorbitant at around US$150 one-way. A handful of local boat operators run occasional trips (try Foster Hopkins on ☎460 0212 or Byron Askie on ☎460 0065) or you could ask around with the charter companies (see p.127).

If you visit independently, getting around is likely to be your major headache. There is no bus service, and distances (and the heat) are sufficient to put all but the hardiest off the idea of walking anywhere. Also, you've no guarantee of finding one of the island's tiny **taxi** fleet in action, so it's worth calling ahead to try to **rent a car** from a private citizen: try Mr Burton (☎460 0103 or 460 0078), Mr Thomas (☎460 0015), Byron Askie (☎460 0065) or Junie Walker (☎460 0159), one of whom can usually oblige for around US$50 per day. Alternatively, ask around at the airport for someone to give you a ride – there's usually a crowd there to meet the flights.

Taking a **day-tour** to the island is the best way to guarantee getting both a driver and a boat operator to take you to the bird sanctuary. Both D&J Forwarders (☎464 3228 or 773 9766) and Jenny's Tours (☎461 9361) will organize a carefully packaged day-tour for US$150, including flights, pick-up at Barbuda airport, a jeep tour of the island, lunch and a boat visit to the bird sanctuary. Your driver will also leave you on the beach for as long as you want – just remember to take a bottle of water. Occasional day-tours by boat are run by Ecoseatours (☎463 0275) and Adventure Antigua (☎560 4672 or 727 3261), both of whom run fast boats to the Barbudan beaches in an hour and a half for snorkelling and beach cruising. Cost around US$120 per person.

For details of accommodation in Barbuda, see p.102; for eating and drinking, see p.117.

CODRINGTON

Map 6, C5.

CODRINGTON, the island's capital and only settlement, holds almost the entire population of 1500 people within its grid of narrow streets. It's a well spread-out place, with plenty of brightly painted single-storey clapboard or concrete buildings. There are a couple of guesthouses, a handful of restaurants, bars and supermarkets, but, for the most part, people keep to themselves, and there is little sign of life apart from a few curious schoolchildren, dogs and the occasional goat. On Sundays the capital livens up with a cricket match at the Holy Trinity School.

Codrington Lagoon

To the west of town, **Codrington Lagoon** is an expansive area of green, brackish water, fringed by mangroves. The

FRIGATE BIRDS

You'll need a boat to get anywhere near the **frigate birds**, motoring out to the edge of the shallows where they live and then poling the boat punt-like to their nests. The sight as you approach is quite spectacular – the mothers will take to the skies as you draw near, joining the multitude of birds wheeling above you, and leaving their babies standing imperiously on the nest but watching you closely out of the corner of their eyes. The display gets even more dramatic during the mating season, from late August to December, when hundreds of the males put on a grand show – puffing up their bright-red throat pouches as they soar through the air just a few metres above the females, watching admiringly from the bushes.

lagoon is completely enclosed on its western side by the narrow but magnificent strip of **Palm Beach**, 22 kilometres long, but there is a narrow cut to the north where fishing boats can get out to the ocean. Lobsters breed in the lagoon and you'll probably see them at the pier being loaded for export to Antigua – an important contribution to the local economy. Equally significant – for this is what is starting to bring in the tourists – a series of mangrove clumps to the northwest of the lagoon, known as **Man of War Island**, provides the home and breeding ground for the largest group of frigate birds anywhere in the Caribbean (see box, above).

Small boats leave for the sanctuary from the main pier just outside Codrington and charge around US$50 per boat. If you just turn up without notice, there is no guarantee that you'll find someone to take you out, so it's advisable to visit as part of a tour or to make arrangements through your hotel or car rental.

AROUND THE ISLAND

To be frank, apart from any beach or snorkelling stops, a tour of the island is a pretty brief affair. Away from the lagoon, there are few "sights" as such – they are certainly not the reason you are here – and they're all pretty missable unless you're determined to get your money's worth.

North of Codrington a series of dirt roads fans out across the upper part of the island. One of these leads into the heart of the island, to the scant remains of **Highlands House**, the castle the first Codringtons built on the island in the seventeenth century. The home must have been pretty extensive, for the ruins – crumbling walls and the occasional piece of staircase – cover a wide area. The views across the island from here are as panoramic as you'll find.

The caves

Map 6, D3 and E4.

Another dirt road leads up to the northeastern side of the island, where a series of **caves** has been naturally carved into the low cliffs. These are thought to have sheltered Taino and possibly Carib Indians in the centuries preceding the arrival of Europeans in the island. Scant evidence of their presence has been found here, however, except for some unusual **petroglyphs**. The entrance to the main cave is opposite a large boulder, with the ruins of an old **watch-tower** built up alongside. You'll need to scramble up the rocks for five minutes, then make a short, stooped walk inside the cave to reach the petroglyphs – a couple of barely distinguishable and very amateurish faces carved into the rockface. What is more noticeable is where pieces of rock have been prised away, a decade or so ago, by tourist vandals eager for their own chunk of ancient art. Alongside the petroglyphs, a large dome-shaped chamber – the "presidential suite" – was probably the main home of the Indians within the complex.

East of these caves, the **Darby Sink Cave** is one of hundreds of sinkholes on the island, dropping seventy feet to a mini-rainforest where palmetto palm trees, shrubs and birds proliferate.

River Fort

Map 6, C6.

You can clamber around some more substantial remains at the **River Fort** in the southwest of the island, just beyond the coconut grove. The fort provides a surprisingly large defence for an island of Barbuda's size and importance. The island was attacked by Carib Indians in the 1680s and by the French navy in 1710, but there was too little valuable property here to tempt any further assailants into braving the dangerous surrounding reefs. As a result, the fort never saw any action, and its main role has been as a lookout and a landmark for ships approaching the island from the south.

The remains are dominated by a **Martello tower**, one of the many built throughout the British Empire during the Napoleonic Wars on the plan of a tower at Cape Mortella in Corsica – hence their name. Right below the tower, the **River Landing** is the main point for access to Barbuda by boat and is always busy with trucks stockpiling and loading sand onto barges to be taken to replenish beaches in Antigua – a controversial but lucrative industry for the Barbudans.

- -
For details on boat trips from Antigua, see p.80.
- -

AROUND THE ISLAND

GREG EVANS

The road into St John's from English Harbour

IAN CUMMING, AXIOM

Rum shop in Jennings

ABBIE ENOCK, TRAVEL INK

Devil's Bridge, on the north coast of Antigua

IAN CUMMING, AXIOM

Military ruins from the British colonial era on Shirley Heights

IAN CUMMING, AXIOM

Driftwood on Ffryes Beach, Antigua

IAN CUMMING, AXIOM

Sunset behind English Harbour

GREG EVANS

A calm, deserted beach on Barbuda

GREG EVANS

Blue striped grunts and snappers amid the offshore coral reefs

BARBUDA'S BEACHES

Invariably deserted, Barbuda's beaches are simply stunning. On the west coast, on the far side of Codrington Lagoon (and so only really accessible by boat), the gently curving Palm Beach offers 22km of dazzling white sand interspersed with long stretches of pink, created by the tiny fragments of millions of seashells washed up over the years. There's little shade here, so ask your boatman to drop you near one of the groves of casuarina trees; he'll come back for you a few hours later.

On the east coast, the attractively named Rubbish Bay and Hog Bay are littered with driftwood and other detritus washed up by the Atlantic Ocean and offer great opportunities for beachcombing, while at many other places around the island you'll spot tiny bays and coves where you can jump out of your car for a private swim and some snorkelling.

Spanish Point

Map 6, G8.

East of here the road leads out past the luxurious *K Club* hotel to the isolated **Spanish Point**, where a small finger of land divides the choppy waters of the Atlantic from the calm Caribbean Sea. Maps indicate a castle on Spanish Point, but if you make the effort to get there all you'll find are the ruins of a small lookout post. More interestingly, there is a marine reserve just offshore at **Palaster Reef**, where numerous shipwrecks have been located in the shallows amid the fabulous coral and abundant reef fish. You can swim to the edges of the reef from the beach, so don't forget your snorkelling or diving gear.

Redonda

The little island of **Redonda** – a two-kilometre hump of volcanic rock rising a sheer 300 metres from the sea – was spotted and named by Columbus in 1493, but subsequently ignored for nearly four centuries. During the 1860s, however, valuable phosphate was found in bird guano there, and Redonda was promptly annexed by Antigua. Mining operations were begun, producing around 4000 tons a year by the end of the century. Output declined after World War I, the mining ceased, and the island has been unoccupied – except by goats and seabirds – since 1930.

Almost surreally, though, Redonda is still claimed as an **independent kingdom**. In 1865 a Montserratian sea-trader Matthew Shiell led an expedition to the island and staked his claim to it. His objections to Antigua's annexation of the island were ignored, but it didn't stop him from abdicating in favour of his novelist son in 1880; he in turn passed the fantasy throne to the English poet John Gawsworth, who took the title Juan III and appointed a number of his friends as nobles of the realm, including Dorothy L. Sayers, J.B. Priestley and Lawrence Durrell. Today, Leo V claims to have inherited the kingdom, using his title to promote the literary works of his predecessors, though at least one pretender to the throne argues that Gawsworth had abdicated in his favour during a night of heavy drinking at his local pub back in England.

Redonda is occasionally visited by yachtsmen – though with no sheltered anchorage, the landing is a difficult one – but there is no regular service to the island, nor anywhere to stay save a few ruined mining buildings when you get there.

LISTINGS

6	Accommodation	89
7	Eating and drinking	103
8	Music and nightlife	118
9	Sports	123
10	Directory	134

Accommodation

Antigua offers plenty of good **accommodation**, but there are also a lot of places that are complacent and overpriced. Prices tend to be high – the country seems to have made a decision to stay relatively "upmarket" in its tourism – which means that you're usually better off arranging accommodation as part of a package in advance.

ACCOMMODATION PRICE CODES

All accommodation listed in this guide has been graded according to the following price categories:

❶ Under US$40   ❷ US$40–60   ❸ US$60–80
❹ US$80–110   ❺ US$110–150   ❻ US$150–200
❼ US$200 and above

Rates are for the cheapest available double or twin room during the high season – normally mid-December to mid-April. During the low season, rates are liable to fall by as much as forty percent (though this is rare at the cheapest places), and proprietors are far more amenable to bargaining. Many of the all-inclusive hotels have a minimum-stay requirement, and rates are quoted per person per night based on double occupancy.

Bear in mind that the prices quoted below are the maximum – particularly outside the winter season, most places will reduce their prices if you plead necessity, and some will do the same all year round. Also keep in mind that every place adds **government tax** of 8.5 percent to the bill and almost all add a **service charge** of ten percent. With some those extras are included in the quoted price; always ask. All places listed are on the beach unless mentioned otherwise.

ST JOHN'S

St John's is a fair way from a decent beach, so the majority of people who stay here are either on business or after the island's cheapest budget accommodation. There are a couple of good-value guesthouses but, if you've got the money, you'll probably prefer to stay out of town near some sand.

City View Hotel
Map 3, F2. Newgate St,
Ⓣe 562 0256, ⒻF 562 0242.
City centre hotel aimed at the business traveller, with 38 comfortable air-conditioned rooms for US$94/83 single, $120/106 double in high/low season. ❺

Heritage Hotel
Map 3, D3. Heritage Quay,
Ⓣ 462 2262, Ⓕ 462 1179.
Right by the cruise-ship pier, this hotel is a decent option if you're in town on business; otherwise, it's completely missable. Spacious if rather

drab rooms, all with their own well-equipped kitchens. ❹

Joe Mike's Hotel
Map 3, E4. Nevis St,
Ⓣ 462 1142, Ⓕ 462 6056.
Just a dozen rooms in this friendly place, right in the centre of town. Again, nothing special but handy if you want to spend a night in the city. Rooms cost US$65 single or double. ❸

Silver Dollar Guest House
Map 3, F7. All Saints/Sheppard streets, Ⓣ 464 3699.

An uninspiring spot but one of the cheapest options on the island, this small and easy-going guesthouse has clean rooms with private baths and fans, a short walk from the market and bus station in downtown St Johns. They charge US$40 for a double, $30 for a single. ❶

ALL-INCLUSIVES

The latest trend in hotel accommodation in the Caribbean has been towards "all-inclusive" hotels, and Antigua is no exception. The simple concept behind these places is that you pay a single price that covers your room, all meals and, normally, all drinks and watersports, so you can "leave your wallet at home". Heavily pushed by travel agents (who take a commission on the total price), all-inclusives really took off in the troubled Jamaica of the 1980s, where many tourists were nervous about leaving their hotel compound at all. Their relevance for an island like Antigua is questionable.

From the local point of view, the problem with all-inclusives is their effect on the independent sector. Local establishments lose custom because guests are tied to their hotel, reluctant to leave it and pay "twice" for food, drink or windsurfing. Nonetheless, all-inclusivity is the flavour of the month in Antigua, with several hotels recently jumping on the bandwagon, and hordes of repeat visitors at places like *Sandals*.

If you're thinking of booking an all-inclusive, focus on what you specifically want out of it. *Sandals* and the giant *Jolly Beach Resort*, for example, have several restaurants and bars, so you don't have to face the same menu every night; smaller places like *Rex Blue Heron* offer less variety, but a bit more space on the beach. Remember, too, that the allure of drinking seven types of "free" cocktail in a night or stuffing your face at the "free" buffet quickly fades, especially if you want to get out and sample Antigua's great restaurants and bars.

ST JOHN'S

THE NORTHWEST COAST

Antigua's **northwest coast** is the most popular destination for visitors, with a series of large and small hotels dotted along the lovely beaches of **Runaway Bay** and **Dickenson Bay**. This is the place to come for action, with plenty of restaurants, watersports and beach life, though you usually only need to walk a short way to find a bit of privacy, even during high season. Badly hit by Hurricane Luis in 1995, Runaway Bay is the quieter of the two, with fewer vendors and a less well-maintained beach. At the northern end of Runaway Bay, around Sunset Cove, the beach is heavily eroded, but prices are dramatically lower and excellent value, and a good beach is only a short walk away.

RUNAWAY BAY

- - - - - - - - - - - - - - - - - - - -

Barrymore Beach Club
Map 4, C5.
ⓣ 462 4101, ⓕ 462 4140,
ⓦ www.vacationspot.com.
A reasonably priced option on a small piece of land with its own tiny, virtually private beach. There's a quiet, secluded feel to the place and the rooms, studios and one-bedroom apartments are comfortable if unspectacular – ask for one close to the sea. The gardens are well-kept and strewn with hibiscus and all types of palm. A reasonable Mexican restaurant is the only eating option on the premises, though a number of others are close by. ④

Island Inn
Map 4, F6. Anchorage Rd,
ⓣ 462 4065, ⓕ 462 4066.
A kilometre or so north of St John's, this small two-storey hotel is curiously located another kilometre from the beach (on Runaway Bay) and targets mostly business travellers, but it's a cosy place with a small pool and good value at US$80/75 for a double room in winter/summer. ④

Lashings
Map 4, A8.

ⓣ 462 4438, ⓕ 462 4491,
ⓦ www.lashings.com.

Good, low-cost and unpretentious option at the southern end of Runaway Bay, with a wide stretch of clean, white beach and decent snorkelling just offshore. The perfectly adequate rooms are rustic and simple, and all fourteen of them face out to sea. There's also a good, reasonably priced beachside restaurant on-site (see p.110). On the downside, the place is a long walk (or a US$6 taxi ride) from any other tourist facilities and the ocean view is marred a bit by the oil-pumping station 3km offshore. Also, it can be noisy: the outdoor bar, which has live entertainment most nights, is open 24 hours a day, and there's also the occasional sunrise party. ❹

Sunset Cove Resort
Map 4, C5.

ⓣ 462 3762, ⓕ 462 2684.
Situated at the northern end of the bay, the hotel has lost its beach entirely in heavy sea swells, and you have to walk five minutes around the headland to swim comfortably. That problem aside, it's a very pleasant place and great value, attractively landscaped with birds nesting in the bougainvillea. There's a small freshwater pool, and the rooms are sizeable and all have kitchen facilities and cable TV. A standard room costs US$80/65 in winter/summer, while the one-bedroom villas that sleep four–six cost US$140/120. ❸

Time Away Apartments
Map 4, C4.

ⓣ 462 0775.
Right next to *Sunset Cove* and suffering from the same beach erosion, this little block offers six decent one-bedroom apartments with tiled floors, rattan furniture (including pull-out couches, so that they can sleep four at a pinch) and self-catering facilities. ❹

THE NORTHWEST COAST

DICKENSON BAY

Antigua Village Condo Beach Resort

Map 4, E3.

Ⓣ 462 2930, Ⓕ 462 0375.
Large if unremarkable resort with dozens of self-catering apartments – from studios to two-bedroom flats – strewn around attractively landscaped gardens. There's a small swimming pool and a grocery store on site, and it's on a good stretch of beach. ❺

Dickenson Bay Cottages

Map 4, G3.

Ⓣ 462 4940, Ⓕ 462 4941,
Ⓦ www.nikegroup.co.uk/antigua
/cottages.htm.
Thirteen spacious, airy and attractively-furnished cottages strewn around a well-landscaped garden and medium-sized pool, up on a hillside overlooking Dickenson Bay. It's a quiet place but just a short walk from the beach and from the much busier *Rex Halcyon Cove*, where guests have subsidized use of the facilities, including tennis and sun-

loungers. One-bedroom cottages cost US$228/155 for two people in winter/summer (US$40 per additional person, though kids stay free), two-bedroom cottages cost US$325 /238 for up to four. ❼

Marina Bay Beach Resort

Map 4, C4.

Ⓣ 462 3254, Ⓕ 462 2151,
Ⓔ marinabay@candw.ag.
Unmistakable salmon-pink buildings overlooking a small marina on the southern edge of Dickenson Bay. The 27 rooms are bright, tastefully furnished and as spacious as you'll find, with good self-catering facilities and cable TV in each. The views over the marina and out to sea are OK, though not as grand as you'll find elsewhere, nor is the beach as good as further north. There are several restaurants a short walk away. ❺

Rex Halcyon Cove

Map 4, G1.

Ⓣ 462 0256, Ⓕ 462 0271,
Ⓦ www.rexcaribbean.com.
Very large, sprawling low-rise resort at the northern end of

the beach, rather faded and a little time-worn but with good-sized rooms, a decent pool and tennis courts and a delightful restaurant on the Warri pier (see p.110). **5**

Sandals Antigua
Map 4, F3.
☎ 462 0267, ℻ 462 4135, ⓦ www.sandals.com.
Part of the popular, all-inclusive chain found throughout the Caribbean, this resort has 189 luxury rooms that are cleverly spread throughout the resort, reducing the sense of being part of a crowd. Four restaurants offer excellent Italian, Japanese, southern US and international food, and all watersports – including diving (training, certification and dives) – are included in the daily rate. Priced from around US$225 per person per day, though (heterosexual) couples only are allowed. **7**

Siboney Beach Club
Map 4, E3.
☎ 462 0806, ℻ 462 3356, ⓦ www.siboneybeachclub.com.

Small, intimate and very friendly place, fabulously landscaped in a micro-jungle of its own. Rooms are spacious and comfortable, and one of the island's best restaurants (*Coconut Grove* – see p.109) is on site. Owner Tony Johnson is a great host and, now in his seventies, still windsurfs daily just offshore. A double room costs from US$190/130 in winter/summer. **6**

Trade Winds Hotel
Map 4, G4.
☎ 462 1223, ℻ 462 5007, ⓦ www.eleganthotels.com.
Lovely place run by Elegant Hotels in the hills above the bay. Air-conditioned rooms are big and comfortable, and guests can chill out by the lagoon pool on a wide veranda overlooking the ocean or take the regular shuttle down to the beach, a kilometre away where sun-loungers are freely available. *The Bay House* restaurant on site (see p.109) is one of the best in the country. Double rooms start at US$205/175 in winter/summer. **7**

THE NORTHEAST

Antigua's **northeast** is pretty quiet from the tourist point of view, with fewer hotels, restaurants, shopping facilities and good beaches than you'll find further west. If you're staying out here, you'll probably want a car – at least for a couple of days – to make up for being so far from the action.

Sunsail Colonna
Map 2, E1. Hodges Bay,
ⓣ 462 6263, ⓕ 462 6430,
ⓦ www.sunsail.com.
Attractive north coast resort, Mediterranean in design – red-tiled roofs and pastel shades throughout – well-landscaped, and with the biggest and most spectacular pool on the island. The beach is pretty ordinary, and you're some way from the island's main action, but the solitude is addictive (though the hotel itself can get quite crowded). Most guests are staying on an all-inclusive package, many taking part in the windsurfing and sailing schools. ❻

EAST COAST

Staying on the **east coast**, you'll feel a long way from any-where – a car is essential for getting out and seeing the island – but the hotels are extremely pleasant and it's very quiet.

Allegro Pineapple Beach Club
Map 2, H3. Long Bay,
ⓣ 463 2006, ⓕ 463 2452.
ⓦ www.allegroresorts.com.
Sprawling but attractively landscaped all-inclusive, with 130 rooms scattered beside a lovely stretch of beach. The place can feel crowded but the facilities – including four tennis courts and free non motorized watersports – are good and there are plenty of activities laid on to distract you. Three restaurants mean you get a bit of variation for your evening meal, and there's a piano bar. ❼

Harmony Hall

Map 2, G5. Brown's Bay,
ⓣ 460 4120, ⓕ 460 4406,
ⓦ www.harmonyhall.com.
A delightful small Italian-run place in the middle of nowhere, open from November to mid-May only. There are six simple but stylish rooms which go for US$150 to $200, with tiled floors, large bathrooms, comfortable beds and small patios. The beach isn't up to much, but a small free boat regularly ferries guests out to the clean white sand at Green Island (see p.57) five minutes away. The restaurant (p.112) is classy and normally busy; when it's closed (as it is most evenings) the hotel lays on separate food for guests. Don't come here for anything other than total peace and quiet. ❻

Long Bay Hotel

Map 2, H3. Long Bay,
ⓣ 463 2005, ⓕ 463 2439,
ⓦ www.longbay-antigua.com.
A small all-inclusive choice located in a fabulous setting by a tiny turquoise bay, with twenty cosy rooms and cottages and a real feeling of isolation. Don't expect anything flash – the hotel owner and his friendly staff pride themselves on keeping everything very low-key and relaxed. There are a few sailboats and windsurfers, plus there's a good tennis court, a big library and a game room with board games. The chef is excellent and the bartender makes the best rum punch on the island. Closed September and October. Rooms start at US$355/267 in high/low season for two, including breakfast and dinner. ❼

ENGLISH HARBOUR AND FALMOUTH

Plenty of good restaurants and nightlife and the proximity of **Nelson's Dockyard** make this an attractive area to stay, though if you're after serious beaches you'll want to look elsewhere on the island.

Admiral's Inn

Map 5, E5. Nelson's Dockyard, ⓣ 460 1153, ⓕ 460 1534. Built in 1788 as the dockyard's supply store and now attractively restored, this is one of the best accommodation options in Antigua, with great atmosphere, welcoming staff, a romantic setting by the harbour and sensible prices. An occasional free boat ferries guests to a nearby beach. ❺

Catamaran Hotel

Map 5, C1. Falmouth, ⓣ 460 1036, ⓕ 460 1506. Friendly little place on the north side of the harbour in Falmouth, adjacent to a small marina. The beach is not great for swimming and it's a bit of a hike to the action at the dockyard, but the rooms are comfortable and good value. ❹

Copper and Lumber Store

Map 5, E5. Nelson's Dockyard, ⓣ 460 1058, ⓕ 460 1529, ⓦ www.antiguanice.com. Very elegant Georgian hotel in the heart of the dockyard, used from the late eighteenth century as its name suggests, with a dozen superb rooms – some fabulously furnished with mostly nautically themed antiques. Quiet at night, but a short walk from a handful of good restaurants. ❻

Falmouth Harbour Beach Apartments

Map 5, D4. Falmouth, ⓣ 460 1027, ⓕ 460 1534. Reasonably sized self-catering studio apartments with ceiling fans and ocean-front verandas on the east side of the harbour by a thin strip of beach. The apartments are nothing spectacular but do offer decent value. ❺

Harbour View Apartments

Map 5, C1. Falmouth, ⓣ 460 1762, ⓕ 460 1871, ⓦ www.antigua-apartments.com. Modern block with a small pool and six two-bed self-catering apartments, all overlooking the harbour, by a small and unexceptional beach. ❺

The Inn on English Harbour

Map 5, F5. English Harbour, ⓣ 460 1014, ⓕ 460 1603, ⓦ www.theinn.ag.

Attractive old hotel, popular with repeat guests and spread over a large site beside the harbour next to a pleasant white-sand beach. There are 22 rooms in a two-storey building bedecked in bougainvillea; prices start at US$320/190 in high/low season. ❼

WEST COAST

Antigua's **west coast** has more hotel rooms than any other part of the island, and a combination of low-, mid- and off-the-scale high-end options to choose from. The *Jolly Beach Resort* and adjoining *Jolly Harbour Villas* form a huge community in the centre of the coast, complete with restaurants, bars and shopping mall, while the southwest has a series of lovely all-inclusives. The Five Islands peninsula, just north of here, has four good hotels in the area, though these feel a little more isolated.

Cocobay Resort

Map 2, D6. Ffryes Beach, ⓣ 562 2400, ⓕ 562 2424, ⓦ www.cocobayresort.com.

Excellent all-inclusive right by the beach, with twenty brightly painted fan-cooled cottages scattered above an impossibly turquoise bay and overlooking the Shekerley Hills. There's a beautiful pool, an aromatherapy /massage treatment room on-site (for which you pay extra) and the food is top-notch. ❼

Curtain Bluff

Map 2, D6. Old Road, ⓣ 462 8400, ⓕ 462 8409, ⓦ www.curtainbluff.com.

For the seriously rich only, a spectacular all-inclusive hotel built on the craggy bluff that overlooks Carlisle Bay and Cades Reef. Rates include all meals and drinks, scuba diving, sailing on the hotel's private yacht and a host of other top-class facilities. ⑦

Galley Bay

Map 2, G3. Five Islands, ⓣ 462 0302, ⓕ 462 4551. Sprouting up between a bird-filled lagoon and a nearly mile-long stretch of beach, this resort is best suited for a romantic retreat. Indeed, none of the seventy rooms, which are mixed nearly evenly between individual thatched-roof cottages and more typical beachside lodging, are equipped with televisions or phones, though bathrobes and private patios are standard. A large lagoon-like pool and two fine restaurants round out the package. All-inclusive rates begin at around US$600 a night during high season. ⑦

Hawksbill Beach

Map 2, C3. Five Islands, ⓣ 462 0301, ⓕ 462 1515, ⓦ www.hawksbill.com. Attractive hotel that sprawls over a vast area on the Five Islands peninsula, overlooking the bay and the jagged rock –

shaped like the beak of a hawksbill turtle – that pokes from the sea and gives the place its name. Four beaches, dramatic views, lovely landscaped gardens and a restored sugar mill converted into a store all add to the atmosphere. Rooms from US$300/165 in winter/summer. ⑦

Jolly Beach Resort

Map 2, C5. Lignum Vitae Bay, ⓣ 462 0061, ⓕ 462 4900. Vast all-inclusive resort – 480 rooms scattered along half a kilometre of good, white beach – with four restaurants, six bars, a disco, a small casino, tennis courts and free watersports (training and rental), including windsurfing, waterskiing, small sailboats and paddle boats. In a place this size, you can't avoid feeling part of a big crowd, and the food is nothing to write home about, but on the whole the place offers pretty decent value. All-inclusive rates per couple start at US$216/190 in winter/summer. ⑦

Jolly Harbour Villas

Map 2, C5. Jolly Harbour,
ⓣ 462 6166, ⓕ 462 6167,
ⓦ www.jollyharbourantigua.com.
Modern complex of about
fifty waterfront villas, mostly
two-bedroom with a full
kitchen and a balcony
overlooking the harbour.
Plenty of shops, restaurants
and sports facilities (including
a golf course and large,
communal swimming pool)
nearby, but the place feels
somewhat bland and
unimaginative. Doubles start
at US$165/135 in
winter/summer. ❻

Rex Blue Heron

Map 2, C6. Johnson's Point,
ⓣ 462 8564,
ⓦ www.rexcaribbean.com.
Medium-sized and very
popular all-inclusive on one
of the best west-coast
beaches, with 64 comfortable
and brightly decorated rooms
and a small pool a stone's
throw from the sea. All-
inclusive rates start at
US$280/260 per room per
night. ❼

Royal Antiguan

Map 2, C3. Deep Bay,
ⓣ 462 3733, ⓕ 462 3732.
At nine storeys this massive
and rather ugly place feels
like a big-city business hotel
accidentally plonked down
in the middle of the
Caribbean. That said, the
facilities are excellent,
particularly for tennis and
watersports, the rooms are
comfortable and the beach
busy but pleasant. If you can
get a decent rate as part of a
package it's not a bad place
to stay if you can handle the
crowd. ❺

Yepton Beach Resort

Map 2, C3. Deep Bay,
ⓣ 462 2520, ⓕ 462 3240,
ⓦ www.yepton.com.
Nothing flash, and not on
Antigua's best beach, but a
pleasantly landscaped and
welcoming little resort, with
its own supply of windsurfers
and small sailboats, and the
occasional bout of
entertainment – live bands,
etc – thrown in for the
guests. The rooms are good
sizes and most have a full
kitchen. ❻

WEST COAST

BARBUDA

Accommodation on the quiet and undeveloped island of **Barbuda** ranges from the rustic to the luxurious, but all of them, whatever the price bracket, offer decent value. Always call ahead to book, and remember to bring mosquito repellent.

K Club
Map 6, E7. Cocoa Point, ⓣ 460 0300, ⓕ 460 0305.
Stunning Italian-owned and designed place in the south of the island, a celebrity home from home with its own golf course and watersports facilities. Prices around US$1200 per room per night. Closed June–Nov. ❼

Nedd's Guesthouse
Map 6, C5. Codrington, ⓣ 460 0059.
Just a handful of comfortable and airy rooms, with a kitchen and grocery store downstairs. If it's full, the owner should be able to direct you to someone who'll

rent you a room, or try Byron Askie on ⓣ 460 0065. ❸

Palmetto Beach Hotel
Map 6, C5.
ⓣ 460 0440, ⓕ 462 0742, ⓦ www.palmettohotel.com.
Smart hotel on a fantastic beach, with 24 beachfront suites all with air-conditioning and a private veranda. The rooms are big, comfortable and stylishly decorated. The chef is Italian and the food excellent, much of it (including the bread and pasta) made fresh on the premises. All-inclusive rates (excluding drinks) start at US$220/170 per person in high/low season. ❼

Eating and drinking

There are plenty of good **eating** options on Antigua and, though prices are generally on the high side, there's usually something to suit most budgets. Around most of the island, hotel and restaurant menus aimed at tourists tend to offer familiar variations on Euro-American style food, shunning local specialities – a real shame, as the latter are invariably excellent and well worth trying if you get the chance.

Some **restaurants** close for a couple of months over the summer, sometimes on a whim, depending on how quiet the season is expected to be. Government tax of 8.5 percent is always added and, particularly at the pricier places, a ten percent service charge is also automatic. **Opening hours** are fairly standard – lunch typically from noon till 2 or 2.30pm, and dinner from 6pm. Bear in mind that many of the smaller restaurants close the kitchen early (around 9pm), particularly when custom is slow.

For **drinking**, Wadadli is the local **beer**, a reasonable brew though not quite a match for the superb Red Stripe – Jamaican beer brewed under licence on the island. Other regular beers on offer include Heineken, Guinness and the Trinidadian Carib. **Rum** is the most popular spirit, used as the basis for a range of cocktails from pina coladas to cuba libre (rum and coke). The English Harbour and Cavalier brands are both made on the island, though real aficionados of the stuff will want to look out for Mount Gay Extra

ANTIGUAN FOOD

Almost everywhere, breakfast is based around coffee, cereal, toast and eggs, and will usually include fresh fruit, one of the country's strong points. Expect to find paw-paws, bananas and the sweet Antiguan black pineapple; in season – generally between May and August – you should also make a special effort to look out for the delicious local mangoes and sapodillas.

For other meals you'll find that seafood – as you'd expect – is one of the island's strongpoints. Of the fish, the tasty and versatile red snapper and grouper are the staples but, if you're lucky, you'll also find swordfish, mahimahi and the very meaty marlin on the menu. Lobster is usually the priciest item, anywhere from EC$45–85 depending on season and the type of establishment. You'll also find conch ("konk") – a large shellfish often curried or battered in fritters, though best of all eaten raw in conch salad, when it's finely chopped with hot and sweet peppers, cucumber and lemon juice – as well as the giant local cockles and whelks, usually served in a buttery garlic sauce.

Other Antiguan specialities include the fabulous ducana (a solid hunk of grated sweet potato mixed with coconut and spices and steamed in a banana leaf), pepperpot stew with salt beef, pumpkin and okra, often served with a cornmeal pudding known as fungi, various types of curry, salted codfish, and souse – cuts of pork marinated in lime juice, onions, hot and sweet peppers and spices.

Vegetarians will find their choices strictly limited – there are some great vegetables grown in Antigua, including pumpkins, okra and the squash-like christophene, but many menus don't include a single vegetarian dish, and even the widely available rice and peas often contains a piece of salted pork.

Old from Barbados or the Haitian Barbancourt, both brilliant Caribbean rums, best served neat on ice.

Of the **soft drinks**, you'll find the usual brands of sodas across the island as well as the tasty sparkling grapefruit drink Ting, made locally. Look out, too, for vendors standing by piles of green coconuts; for a couple of EC dollars they'll cut the top off one for you to drink the sweet, delicious milk.

Finally, if you're heading to Barbuda, don't expect the same level of choice and sophistication as you do on Antigua. Away from the posh hotels, restaurants and bars are low-key and, like the island's pace of life, exceedingly slow.

ST JOHN'S

Although you most likely won't be staying in **St John's**, there's plenty of reason to head into town when it comes to chow-time. The city has a number of good restaurants, many of them scattered around Redcliffe Quay, offering a nice range of options.

RESTAURANT PRICES AND RESERVATIONS

In the reviews that follow, restaurants have been graded as inexpensive (under US$20 a head for a three-course meal without drinks), moderate (US$20–30), expensive (US$30–40) and very expensive (over US$40). During the winter season (Dec–April) it's worth making a reservation at many of the places recommended and, if you've got your heart set on a special place, arrange it a couple of days in advance if you can. And finally, a word on prices; some restaurants quote their prices in EC$, others in US$, others in both. We've followed their practice, using whichever currency a particular restaurant quotes. Remember that US$1 is worth EC$2.70.

Bliss Sports Cafe

Map 3, E2. Lower Church St,
Ⓣ 562 2796.

Daily 11am–late. Inexpensive
–moderate.

Popular sports bar, where
crowds gather for both live
and taped international sport
– from international cricket
and boxing to English
Premiership football – and
munch on daily specials like
fungi and saltfish or bullfoot
stew (both EC$13). There's a
variable entry charge for
major events/games.

Candyland

Map 2, C3. Fort James.

Daily. Inexpensive–moderate.
Friendly little beach bar
under the casuarina trees just
before you reach Fort James
serving good, simple food all
day. Regular specials include
various curries, steamed fish
and conch chowder.

Chutneys

Map 2, D3. Fort Rd,
Ⓣ 462 2977.

Tues–Sun dinner only; closed
Mon. Moderate.
The only authentic Indian
restaurant on the island, five-

minutes' drive north of
town between *KFC* and
Pizza Hut, serving a wide
variety of chicken, lamb and
seafood curries – from mild
to highly spicy – as well as
tandoori, tikka, rotis and
some excellent vegetable
dishes. There's also a large
non-curry menu that
includes the bizarre
sounding but popular mako
shark in champagne sauce
(US$15).

Commissioner's Grill

Map 3, D3. Redcliffe Quay.
Ⓣ 462 1883.

Daily. Moderate.
Excellent West Indian food is
served all day in this popular
and easy-going saloon, from
tasty breakfasts of saltfish,
eggs or fruit through to
hearty suppers of fish,
chicken and lobster.

Hemingway's

Map 3, D3. St Mary's St,
Ⓣ 462 2763.

Mon–Sat 8.30am–11pm; closed
Sun. Moderate–expensive.
Atmospheric, early
nineteenth-century green-
and-white wooden building

ST JOHN'S

with a balcony overlooking the street and Heritage Quay. Can be overwhelmingly popular when the cruise ships are in; at other times it's a great place to be, serving a range of excellent food from sandwiches and burgers to fish and steak dinners.

Home Restaurant
Map 2, D3. Lower Gambles, ⊤ 461 7651.
Mon–Sat dinner only; lunch also on Sat; closed Sun. Expensive.
Attractive restaurant in a converted home, a little way from the centre of town, serving great, adventurous West Indian food. Look for starters of roast peppers and beets in balsamic vinegar and garlic (EC$18), main courses of mahimahi with plantain mousse (EC$60) or blackened redfish (EC$55).

Joe Mike's
Map 3, E4. Nevis St/Corn Alley, ⊤ 462 1142.
Daily 7.30am–10pm.
Inexpensive.
Unpretentious local eatery that's also a small hotel and a popular lunchtime haunt for government ministers and other prominent Antiguans. Servings include large portions of ducana and saltfish, stewed pork, fungi and lingfish or barbecued ribs, all for around EC$15–25.

Millers by the Sea
Map 2, C3. Fort James.
⊤ 462 9414.
Daily. Moderate–expensive.
Large beachside restaurant a kilometre or so north of St John's, with an extensive menu and live music every night (see p.120). Typical dishes include curried conch or pan-fried snapper for US$18/EC$48, and there's normally a beach barbecue for lunch and dinner on Thursday.

Papa Zouk
Map 2, D3. Hilda Davis Drive, Gambles,
⊤ 562 1284.
Weds–Sat 6pm–11pm (Nov–April Mon–Sat).
Moderate–expensive.
Imaginative Antiguan food served on a tiny patio festooned with flowers. The menu is small but interesting,

ST JOHN'S

with local produce thrown into dishes like Creole bouillabaisse or a seafood medley.

Pizzas in Paradise

Map 3, D4. Redcliffe Quay. ☎ 480 6985. Closed Sun. Moderate.

Pub-like atmosphere, popular with tourists for lunch and dinner, serving reasonable quality food inside or outdoors under the trees at decent prices – pizzas, salads and baked potatoes as well as more typical Antiguan fish

and chicken meals from EC$15–35.

The Redcliffe Tavern

Map 3, D4. Redcliffe Quay. ☎ 461 4557. Mon–Sat 8am–9pm. Moderate.

Housed in one of the renovated quayside warehouses, the atmospheric tavern serves good American/Caribbean food all day, with options such as flying fish in beer batter, jerk chicken, Creole shrimp and pan-fried mahimahi fish all for around US$15.

THE NORTH AND EAST

With a wide range of hotels dotted around the **north coast** there is a steady stream of punters looking for good places to eat, and plenty of decent restaurants have popped up as a result, though there are few options in the low-budget range. **Dickenson Bay** has the widest choice but, if you're staying around the coast in the northeast, you'll need to travel a bit if you want to vary your options. Further **east**, the hotels are all-inclusive so, with all the guests already catered for, there is virtually no room for an independent restaurant. Accordingly, don't plan to eat dinner out there unless you want to buy an evening pass to one of the hotels. Lunch at *Harmony Hall*, on the other hand, is an excellent option.

RUNAWAY BAY AND DICKENSON BAY

Bay House

Map 4, G4. *Trade Winds Hotel*, ☎ 462 1223.

Daily 7am–10pm.

Expensive–very expensive.

Smart restaurant on an airy terrace high on the hill overlooking Dickenson Bay, and an ideal and romantic place for a drink at sunset followed by top-class food. Tasty and creative starters set the tone – pork and prawn wontons or conch marinated in lime cost US$10–12 – while main courses might include pan-fried kingfish with a pepper salsa for US$20 or fillet of beef marinated in soy sauce with Chinese cabbage for US$26. Save room for dessert – the chocolate *millefeuille* with raspberry sauce (US$9) is beyond superlatives.

The Beach

Map 4, E3. Dickenson Bay, ☎ 480 6940.

Daily 8.30am–midnight.

Moderate–expensive.

Newly refurbished and brightly painted restaurant on the beach right by the *Antigua Village Hotel*, serving good food all day. Lunches include sushi, satay, burgers and salads for US$8-10; dinner specials might be sesame-crusted tuna, meaty pasta or seafood stew for US$20–30.

Coconut Grove

Map 4, E3. *Siboney Beach Club*, Dickenson Bay, ☎ 462 1538.

Daily for lunch and dinner.

Expensive–very expensive.

One of the top food choices on the island, as the great cooking and friendly service are added to by the delightful open-air beachside location. Mouthwatering starters include deep-fried jumbo shrimp in a coconut dip (US$12.50) and seafood gumbo (US$7), while main courses feature dishes like mahimahi in a mango salsa (US$23) and rock lobster in Creole sauce (US$23). Desserts include a magnificent coconut cream pie for US$9.25.

THE NORTH AND EAST

Lashings
Map 4, A8. Runaway Bay,
☎ 462 4438.
Daily for breakfast, lunch and
dinner. Moderate.
With a massive menu, 24-
hour bar and pizzas until
4am, this beachside place at
Lashings Hotel always seems
busy. Pizzas start at EC$16,
while dishes of blackened
swordfish, barbecued chicken,
shrimp curry or cottage pie
range from EC$25 to $45.

If you're craving a round of fish (or sausage) and chips,
look out for the fast-food van parked out on the main road
between the *Marina Bay Hotel* and *Siboney Hotel* most
Wednesdays and Fridays from around 4.30–9.30pm.
A basket of fried fish will run you EC$25.

The Lobster Pot
Map 4, C6. Runaway Bay,
☎ 462 2855.
Daily 7.30am–midnight.
Moderate–expensive.
Good food served all day on
a large beachfront covered
veranda at the back of the old
Runaway Bay Hotel,
devastated by Hurricane Luis,
but still overlooking a lovely
stretch of sand. Efficient and
unobtrusive staff offer lunches
of blackened fish, shrimp and
chicken linguine for US$12–
15 or more basic sandwiches
and salads for US$7–10,
while the evening meals
include thick soups for
US$5–7.50, catch of the day
for US$21 and various lobster
options starting at US$30.

Pari's Pizza
Map 4, G3. Dickenson Bay,
☎ 462 1501.
Tues–Sun 6–11pm. Moderate.
Pizzas, ribs and steaks –
nothing earth-shattering, and
slightly overpriced at EC$50
for a small rack of ribs,
EC$24 for the smallest of the
pizzas, EC$69 for some surf
and turf, but reasonable
enough if you're staying
nearby.

Warri Pier
Map 4, F2. *Rex Halcyon Cove*,
Dickenson Bay,

ⓣ 462 0256.

Daily for lunch and dinner.
Moderate–expensive.

Delightful open-air dining on a pier jutting out into the bay, with an option of sitting at small tables along the boardwalk or at the end of the pier. American staples dominate the lunch menu, with burgers and BLTs for US$7–12, with a more interesting evening selection of fresh fish and steaks at US$15–25.

NORTHEAST

The Coast

Map 2,E1. Next to *Sunsail Colonna*, Hodges Bay,
ⓣ 462 6263.

Daily for lunch and dinner.
Moderate–expensive.

Rock solid oceanside restaurant, catering principally for the adjoining *Sunsail* hotel. Starters include fried brie, baked breadfruit and conch salad for US$10–12, and mains of garlic and basil polenta, rack of lamb or skewered king prawns for US$14–26.

Le Bistro,

Map 2, E1. Hodges Bay,
ⓣ 462 3881.

Tues–Sat dinner only; closed Mon. Expensive–very expensive.

Long-established and well-reputed restaurant with a calm vibe and good, unobtrusive service, laying on excellent, authentic French food including starters of onion soup for EC$20 and snails in garlic butter for EC$25, main courses of lobster fettucine (EC$55), stir-fried shrimps flambéed in brandy (EC$70) and duck in orange sauce (EC$65).

EAST COAST

The Beach Bar

Map 2, G4. Long Bay.

Daily for lunch only.
Inexpensive.

Often lively local spot right on the beach that makes for a great place to take a break from the sun and surf. Chicken and rice, burgers or fish and chips for EC$15–25.

THE NORTH AND EAST

meal includes free boat trip

Harmony Hall

Map 2, G5. Nonsuch Bay,
☎ 460 4120.
Daily 10am–6pm; Fri & Sat
dinner also. Closed May–Nov.
Expensive.

Run by a charming Italian
couple, this is one of the
island's finer restaurants, even if
it is set in the middle of
nowhere. Built around an old
sugar mill, the elegant but
simple food is served on a
terrace overlooking the bay.
Starters include pumpkin soup,
lobster bisque and coconut
shrimp for EC$18/25/35,
mains of lobster ravioli or
catch of the day for
EC$38/55, and delicious
desserts of crème brulee or
deep-fried bananas in
cinnamon for EC$18. Despite
the long drive and the poor-
condition road, it's always busy
and well worth the trip.

ENGLISH HARBOUR AND AROUND

Most of the good **south-coast** restaurants are concentrated
around **Nelson's Dockyard** and nearby **Falmouth
Harbour**. Two others to look out for are *Albertos* – a five-
minute drive or taxi-ride away – and the *Lookout*, high up
on Shirley Heights.

Abracadabra

Map 5, E4. Nelson's Dockyard,
☎ 460 2701.
Daily 6–11pm.
Moderate–expensive.
Just outside the dockyard and
offering a mostly Italian
menu of pastas and grilled
meat and fish, with a cosy
atmosphere and live music
several nights a week (see
p.121).

The Admiral's Inn

Map 5, E5. Nelson's Dockyard,
☎ 460 1027.
Daily 7am–9pm. Moderate.
Good, unpretentious dining
in the old building or, more
romantically, by the water's
edge (take mosquito
repellent), with the
occasional local dishes among
the more standard meals of
fish, chicken and salads.

Albertos

Map 2 F6. Willoughby Bay,
ⓣ 460 3007.
Tues–Sun dinner only; closed
July–Oct. Expensive. ⤙

Probably the best food on the
south coast, hosted by the
eponymous longtime
proprietor at an out of the
way spot. The evening's food
is chalked up on a
blackboard; recurring entries
include thin slices of
breadfruit roasted in a garlic
and parsley sauce (EC$25)
and pan-fried tuna or wahoo
with wasabi and ginger
(EC$60). Top desserts send
you happily on your way.

Dockyard Bakery

Map 5, E5. Nelson's Dockyard.
Daily 8am–5pm. Inexpensive.

Nice place for breakfast or
daytime snacks, selling guava
Danishes, pineapple turnovers
and bread pudding, all freshly
baked in the dockyard's old
kitchens.

Eden Café

Map 5, E5. Nelson's Dockyard,
ⓣ 460 2701.
Daily 8.30am–4pm.
Inexpensive–moderate.

Friendly little place next to
Abracadabra, serving tasty and
healthy shakes, smoothies and
salads as well as huge
baguettes and sandwiches
(EC$20–25) and fine coffee.

Famous Mauro's

Map 5, E1. Cobbs Cross,
ⓣ 460 1318.
Daily for lunch and dinner.
Moderate.

Probably the best place for
pizza on Antigua, with more
than thirty types available
daily, all freshly cooked in the
wood-burning oven.

HQ

Map 5, E5. Nelson's Dockyard.
Daily for lunch and dinner.
Moderate–expensive.

Excellent place in the heart of
the dockyard, where an
Australian chef creates
imaginative Asian/Caribbean
fusion food. Starters at
US$7–10 include Thai squid
salad and sashimi; main dishes
of hot and sweet fish (US$17),
chilli lamb (US$23) or lobster
that you choose from the tank
(US$27). The menu is similar
at lunch-time, though cheaper
snacks are also on offer.

Jackee's Kwik Stop

Map 5, E4. Falmouth Harbour.
Daily for lunch and dinner.
Inexpensive.
One of the best of the local eateries run by the delightful Jackee, this little café sells typical Antiguan food, with daily specials of ducana and saltfish, pepperpot and fungi or souse.

The Last Lemming

Map 5, D4. Falmouth Harbour, ☎ 460 6910.
Daily for lunch and dinner.
Moderate.
Good food at this frequently crowded harbourside spot, though the service can be dreadfully slow. Pan-fried catch of the day and grilled steaks are typical of the daily offerings.

The Lookout

Map 5, G6. Shirley Heights, ☎ 460 1785.
Daily 10am–6pm. Moderate.
The only place for a refreshment break while you're up on the Heights, with a large patio providing superb views over the harbour and the dockyard. Simple meals are the order of the day, with the Sunday (and, to a lesser extent, Thurs) barbecues pulling a huge crowd for the reggae and steel bands that play from early afternoon through to the late evening (see p.122).

The Mad Mongoose

Map 5, E4. Falmouth Harbour.
Tues–Sun 10am–11pm.
Moderate.
Often lively bar, absolutely packed when the boats are in, serving snacks and simple meals a stone's throw from the water.

WEST COAST

As well as a series of eateries lined up along the marina at **Jolly Harbour**, this side of the island offers a handful of places dotted along the coast, including a couple of small but good-value beach bars and – in *Chez Pascal* and *Cocos* – two isolated but quality restaurants.

v. expensive
and gd.

WEST COAST

Al Porto

Map 2, C5. Jolly Harbour,
℡ 462 7695.
Daily 11.30am–2.30pm &
6–10.30pm. Moderate.
Popular Italian open-air
eatery, in a lovely spot right
by the marina, with starters
of mozzarella and tomatoes or
chunky soups for US$5–8,
standard pastas for US$7–15,
solid pizzas for US$10–15,
grilled fish or steaks for
US$20–25 and lobster for
US$30.

Chez Pascal _not gd + expensive_

Map 2, C3. Galley Bay Hill,
Five Islands, ℡ 462 3232.
Mon–Sat for lunch and dinner.
Expensive.
Good French restaurant
serving classy food in an
intimate and cosy setting. It's
well out of the way on the
Five Islands peninsula, with
attractive views over the area
and out to sea. Pass the
Galley Bay Hotel, take a right
and then go right again up a
steep hill.

Cocos v. nice setting

Map 2, C5. Lignum Vitae Bay,
℡ 462 9700.
oh food.

Daily for lunch and dinner.
Expensive.
One of the most romantic
spots on the island – a
candlelit terrace overlooking
a gorgeous west-coast bay –
and the food's pretty good,
too. Look for starters of
pumpkin soup, conch fritters
or crab cakes for EC$12–16,
and main courses of baked
tuna with red peppers or
grouper fillet with lime for
EC$42–45.

Dogwatch Tavern

Map 2, G5. Jolly Harbour,
℡ 462 6550.
Bar open daily 11am–10pm,
Sat & Sun 5–10pm. Restaurant
daily from 6pm.
Inexpensive–moderate.
English-style pub with pool
tables and dartboards,
decorated with flags,
pennants and sailing regalia,
right beside the marina, with
tables indoors and out.
There's an inexpensive
outdoor snack-bar and grill,
with burgers for EC$20, hot
dogs for EC$10, red snapper
with peas and rice for
EC$28, and an 8oz NY strip
steak with fries for EC$45.

WEST COAST

Peter's

Map 2, C5. Jolly Harbour.
Daily 8–11am, noon–2.30pm & 6–10pm. Moderate–expensive.
Heavily meat-oriented barbecue zone overlooking the marina, with reasonable if unspectacular offerings. Daily lunch specials like chicken and chips or sandwiches for just EC$15; dinners of seafood kebabs with rice or veal in cream sauce cost around EC$50, and there's an open salad bar (EC$22).

Steely Bar

Map 2, C5. Jolly Harbour, ☎ 462 6260.
Daily 8am–late. Moderate.
Food is offered all day at this lively place, overlooking the marina in the heart of the Jolly Harbour complex, 250 metres along the boardwalk from the *Al Porto* restaurant. A full English or American breakfast will set you back EC$23, while an extensive lunch menu features various salads (EC$19–27), hot dogs and burgers. Dinner options might include pan-fried duck breast (EC$52) or Cajun snapper with rice (EC$43).

There's entertainment every night also (see p.122). Close by, and free for residents of the nearby villas, there's a big and popular pool as well as tennis and squash courts; visitors can buy a pass.

Turner's Beach Bar & Grill

Map 2, C6. Johnson's Point, ☎ 462 9133.
Daily 11am–9pm.
Inexpensive–moderate.
Delightful little restaurant on another of the best west-coast beaches, a stone's throw from the *Blue Heron Hotel*. It's an unpretentious place, with plastic furniture right on the sand, but the cooking is good and the atmosphere mellow. The evening menu includes chicken curry (US$11), grilled red snapper (US$14), shrimp in pineapple (US$15) and grilled lobster (US$22), as well as vegetable or chicken rotis (US$7). During the day, you'll find the same menu, but even if you're not particularly hungry, it's a great place to retreat from the beach for a snack and a beer. Worth calling ahead for a reservation at night.

BARBUDA

Restaurants in **Barbuda** are low-key places, with quiet trade. If you're coming on a day-trip package your meal will normally be arranged for you, but if you're making your own arrangements it's worth giving as much advance notice as you can so that they can get the ingredients in.

Green Door Tavern

Map 6, C5. Codrington.

Daily 11am–9pm. Inexpensive.

Good low-cost local food, with a barbecue on Friday and Saturday evenings and an easy-going vibe at all times.

K Club

Map 6, E7. Coco Point, ☏ 460 0300.

Daily lunch and dinner. Very expensive.

Spectacular place, beautifully designed and furnished and set on an exquisite beach. Except at busy times, anyone visiting the island is welcome for lunch and dinner, but call ahead to book. Expect great food, beautiful people, a fabulous setting and hefty prices.

Lagoon Café

Map 6, C5. Codrington, ☏ 460 0439.

Daily lunch and dinner. Inexpensive.

The main nightly hangout, a dimly lit place offering simple meals like steamed grouper or curried chicken with peas and rice, guys playing dominos and the (very) occasional live band.

Palm Tree

Map 6, C5. Codrington, ☏ 460 0395.

Daily for lunch. Moderate.

Good island food, particularly for fish and lobster, but you'll need to let them know that you're coming (preferably a day in advance) and what you want to eat.

BARBUDA

Music and nightlife

As you'd expect with Antigua's small population, the country doesn't offer a vast amount in the way of regular nightlife. There are only a couple of **nightclubs** on the island, one cinema and no regular theatres, though some of the best bars lay on occasional live **music**. We've listed the most likely places below, but you'll want to keep an eye open for flyers and radio and newspaper ads announcing where the live bands are going to be. If you're here in July/August, you'll find that the country's annual **Carnival** (see box, opposite) more than compensates for the quiet times.

ST JOHN'S AND THE NORTH

Casino Riviera

Map 4, D5. Runaway Bay, ☎ 562 6262.
Sun–Thurs 10am–2am, Fri & Sat 10am–4am.
Small, air-conditioned casino which, while it can't be claimed as the most inspiring place on the island, offers plenty of gambling opportunities at blackjack, roulette, sports betting and slots.

Deluxe Cinema

Map 3, F3. High St, St John's, ☎ 462 2188.
The island's only cinema, showing the latest imports from the USA.

CARNIVAL

The highlight of Antigua's entertainment calendar is its **Carnival**, a colourful, exuberant party held for ten days, from late July until the first Tuesday in August. Warm-ups start in early July, with steel bands, Calypsonians and Deejays in action across the island, and carnival proper gets cracking with the opening of Carnival City at the Antigua Recreation Ground in St John's. This is where all of the scheduled events take place, though you'll often find spontaneous outbreaks of partying across the city, and a festival village is set up nearby to provide space for the masses of food and drink vendors who emerge out of nowhere.

The major carnival events take place over the last weekend and you'll have to cancel sleep for a few days of frantic action. The **Panorama** steelband contest (Fri night) and the Calypso Monarch competition (Sun night) are both packed and definitely worth catching, while on the Monday morning – the day on which the islands celebrate slave emancipation in 1834 – **Jouvert** (pronounced *jouvay*, and meaning daybreak) is a huge jump-up party starting at 4am. The Judging of the Troupes and Groups competition in the afternoon sees ranks of brightly costumed marching bands and floats parading through the city streets, being marked for colour, sound and general party attitude.

Tuesday has a final costumed parade through the streets, finishing with the announcement of all of the winners and a roughly 6pm–midnight last lap from Carnival City – "the bacchanal" – as the exhausted partygoers stream through St John's, led by the steelbands. All in all, it's a great event – certainly one of the best of the Caribbean's summer carnivals – and a great chance to catch the Antiguans in a nonstop party mood.

King's Casino
Map 3, D3. Heritage Quay, St John's, ☎ 462 1727.
Mon–Sat 10am–4am, Sun 6pm–4am.

The city's main casino, packed with slot machines and offering blackjack, roulette and Caribbean stud poker tables for the more serious players. Live bands and karaoke give the place a bit of atmosphere after 10pm. The casino will normally lay on one-way shuttle services to St John's for those coming to gamble for the night. It'll pick you up anywhere, but you're stuck with the taxi fare home.

Lashings

Map 4, A8. Runaway Bay, ☎ 462 4438.
Open nightly. Small cover charge.

With a stage set up by the 24-hour bar of the *Lashings* hotel (see p.93) the place rocks with live local bands on Friday and Saturday evenings and, during holidays, test matches and Carnival, pretty much every night.

Millers by the Sea

Map 2, C3. Fort James, St John's, ☎ 462 9414.
One of the best venues on the island, this large and often lively restaurant and bar has live music every night varying from local jazz

and soca bands to guitarists and karaoke. Look out, too, for special events here on the big outdoor sets: during 2001 *Millers* hosted Shaggy, as well as a big Calypso fest with Trinidad's Shadow David Rudder that coincided with the annual test match. For special events, there's a cover charge – normally between EC$30 and $50.

Outback

Map 4, E4. Putters, Dickenson Bay, ☎ 560 4653.
Wed, Fri & Sat from 7pm. Small cover charge.

Brand new nightclub favouring Europop and Caribbean classics (plus the occasional live band) aimed at (and attracting) more in the way of tourists than Antiguans.

Ribbit

Map 2, C3. Green Bay, St John's, ☎ 462 7996.
10.30pm–5am Fri and Sat. EC$20.

Ribbit is the island's main nightclub, popular with Antiguans and tourists alike

go beyond to beach bar. → hich.

THE SWEETEST MANGO

Antigua's first full-length feature movie, *The Sweetest Mango*, was shot entirely on location during 2000, and made a good impression on international film festivals during 2001. Written by local author **Gisele Isaac**, and featuring an Antiguan and wider Caribbean cast, it tells the poignant story of thirty-year-old Lovelyann's return to her home country after two decades in Canada.

Filmed all around the island – from Devil's Bridge in the west to Redcliffe Quay and the *Ribbit* nightclub in St John's – and thumping with a local soundtrack, it's great entertainment, particularly for anyone with an interest in the island.

and absolutely packed at the weekends. Music ranges from Jamaican dancehall to Eurosmooch, and the atmosphere is invariably welcoming. It's just off the main road between St John's and Five Islands – follow the road out of St John's that hugs the south side of the harbour and keep going for about a kilometre.

Russell's

Map 2, C3. Fort James, St John's, ⊤ 462 5479.
Mellow jazz outdoors at this small but attractively located restaurant and bar on Friday nights from around 8pm.

ENGLISH HARBOUR AND THE SOUTH

- - - - - - - - - - - - - - - - - - - -

Abracadabra

Map 5, E4. English Harbour, ⊤ 460 2701.
7–11pm nightly. No cover charge.
Welcoming place with Deejays and occasional live bands getting patrons up for some open-air dancing on a small dance floor next to the restaurant (see p.112).

Hype

Map 5, E5. English Harbour, ⊤ 562 2354.
Wed–Sun 7pm–1am. No cover charge.

New, loud nightclub and bar on a pier over the water, with Deejays in the week and bands at the weekends. Popular with both the sailing crowd and locals.

The Last Lemming

Map 5, D4. Falmouth Harbour, ⓣ460 6910.
Open nightly. No cover charge. Lively bar, often open later than anywhere else and with the occasional local band.

The Lookout

Map 5, G6. Shirley Heights
Thurs and Sun from 4pm. No cover charge.
Steel and reggae bands set up on the Heights on Sunday and (less crowded) Thursday afternoons, overlooking English Harbour. There's a bar and barbecue, vendors selling trinkets and T-shirts and a great party atmosphere, though at the peak of the season you'll find little room to move.

THE WEST COAST

Royal Antiguan

Map 2, C3. Five Islands, ⓣ462 3733.
Open nightly. No cover charge. Normally the liveliest spot on the Five Islands peninsula (and open to outsiders), the hotel has a small disco and a casino area with pool tables, slots and video games.

Steely Bar

Map 2, C5. BBR Sportive, Jolly Harbour, ⓣ462 6260.
Open nightly. No cover charge. The main entertainment zone for the Jolly Harbour area, with large TV screens showing sports matches, a steel band on Friday nights, karaoke on Saturday, movies on Sunday and always a crowd of people milling around.

Sports

The confirmed beach addict and the watersports fanatic are equally at home in Antigua, with a variety of great beaches to choose from and plenty of operators offering excellent **diving**, **snorkelling**, **waterskiing** and other activities. Also on the water, a number of companies offer **trips along the coast** by boat or catamaran, and you can charter boats for **deep-sea fishing**. There are plenty of land-based options, too, with a couple of good **golf** courses, a **horse-riding** stable and **hiking** and **mountain-biking** trips.

Although diving options around Antigua are best in the south, the northwest coast is probably the best spot for general watersports, with Dickenson Bay in particular offering several reputable operators at its northern end. The sea is pretty calm here year round and, beyond the protected swimming zone, you can waterski, windsurf, parasail or jetski. **Paradise Reef**, a half-kilometre-long coral garden to the north of the bay, is a popular spot for glass-bottom boat trips and snorkelling, and there are good coralheads offshore around tiny **Prickly Pear Island** a short boat-ride to the northeast.

Barbuda surpasses even Antigua in the quality (and quietness) of its beaches, and its snorkelling and diving opportunities are also world-class. Unfortunately, the island has little in the way of infrastructure to support tourists looking for watersports and you may have to take your own gear.

DIVING AND SNORKELLING

Diving is excellent on the coral reefs around Antigua and Barbuda, with most of the good sites – places like Sunken Rock and Cape Shirley – on the south side of the larger island and many of them very close to shore, rarely more than a fifteen-minute boat-ride away. Expect to see a wealth of fabulously colourful reef fish, including parrot fish, angelfish, wrasse and barracuda, as well as the occasional harmless nurse shark and, if you're lucky, dolphins and turtles. The reefs for the most part are still in pristine, unspoiled condition, and, though there is no wall diving and most dives are fairly shallow, there are some good cliffs and canyons and a handful of wrecks.

Antigua has plenty of reputable dive operators scattered conveniently around the island, so you should always be able to find a boat going out from near where you're staying. Rates are pretty uniform: reckon on around US$50 for a single-tank dive, US$70 for a two-tank dive and US$60 for a night dive. Beginners can get a feel for diving by taking a half-day **resort course**, involving basic theory, a shallow water (or pool) demonstration and a single dive. The course costs around US$80–100, and allows you to continue to dive with the people who taught you, though not with any other operator. Full **open-water certification** – involving theory, tests, training dives and four full dives – is rather more variable in price, costing US$300–500, depending on the time of year and how busy the operator is. Call around for the best deal.

Serious divers should consider a **package deal**, either

involving a simple three or five two-tank dive package (roughly US$180–200 and US$265–300 respectively) or a deal that includes accommodation and diving. Prices for these can be pretty good value, particularly outside the winter season and it's worth contacting the dive operators direct to find out the latest offers.

Barbuda's diving is at least as good as Antigua's, with countless wrecks dotted around the nearby reefs, but, sadly, there is no established dive outfit on the island. At the time of writing, the *Palmetto Beach Hotel* (see p.102) was planning to offer diving for guests but not (yet) for visitors, so if you're interested it's worth asking some of the Antiguan dive operators for the latest information. Or, check with one of the agencies that offers tours to the island – they can normally arrange for certified divers to be provided with tanks and guides on Barbuda, though the costs can be hefty.

Snorkelling around the islands is excellent, too, and several of the dive operators take snorkellers on their dive trips, mooring near some good, relatively shallow coralheads. Reckon on around US$15–20 for an outing, including equipment, though if you're with a friend who's diving you may be able to blag yourself a free trip. However, a boat-ride is far from essential for snorkellers – there are loads of good spots just a short swim offshore from both Antigua and Barbuda, and these are mentioned throughout the *Guide*. Most of the top hotels have snorkelling gear for hire or loan, but if you're not at one of these, finding the equipment can be tricky (try *Deep Bay Divers* in St John's), and it's worth bringing a mask and fins with you, certainly if you're heading to Barbuda.

Aquanauts

Map 2, F6. *St James Club*, Mamora Bay, ☎ 460 5000.

Good, professional south-coast outfit with top-quality equipment, catering for the hotel guests and drop-ins from elsewhere.

Deep Bay Divers

Map 3, D4. Redcliffe Quay, St James, ⓣ 463 8000, ⓦ www.deepbaydivers.com. Rather new outfit with a 34ft dive boat with room for up to fourteen divers and offering trips down to Cades Reef in the southwest (a fifty-minute ride) or straight out to Sandy Island fifteen-minutes' west of St John's. Snorkellers welcome if there's room; gear costs US$10 to rent.

Dive Antigua

Map 4, G1. *Rex Halcyon Cove Hotel*, Dickenson Bay, ⓣ 462 3483, ⓕ 462 7787. The longest established and best-known dive operation on the island, based on the northwest coast, though prices are normally a little higher than most of the others. They offer a glass-bottomed boat to take snorkellers out to the reef.

Dockyard Divers

Map 5, E5. Nelson's Dockyard, ⓣ 460 1178, ⓕ 460 1179. Decent-sized dive shop (and the only outfit in the English Harbour area offering snorkelling tours) that lays on diving trips around the south and west coasts.

Jolly Dive

Map 2, C5. Jolly Harbour Marina, ⓣ 462 8305. Second-oldest dive shop in Antigua and very popular with guests at the big, local hotels; look elsewhere if you want to go out in a small group.

Octopus Divers

Map 5, C1. English Harbour, ⓣ 460 6286, ⓕ 463 8528, ⓦ www.octopusdivers.com. Reputable outfit with one of the most comfortable dive boats on the south coast, and some good-value hotel /diving package deals from time to time – check their Web site for details.

BOATS AND CATAMARANS

There is no shortage of **boat and catamaran trips** to be made around Antigua, with the emphasis – not, it must be said, everyone's cup of tea – normally on being part of a big crowd all having a fun time together. Most of the cruises charge a single price, including a meal and all the drinks you want, and the two main cruise companies, Kokomo and Wadadli Cats, offer virtually identical trips, travelling on large and comfortable catamarans. A more interesting and unusual **ecotour** is offered by Adventure Antigua.

The most popular cruise – a great way to see the island – sails right round Antigua, taking in some snorkelling and lunch at Green Island off the east coast. There is also a superb snorkelling trip to Cades Reef on the south coast, stopping off for lunch on one of the west-coast beaches, and another to uninhabited Great Bird Island – where there's plenty of birdlife – off the northeast. Finally, there's a "triple destination" cruise on Sundays to English Harbour via Green Island, ending with a taxi-ride up to the steel band party on Shirley Heights and another taxi home.

Each of the trips is offered by Kokomo and Wadadli, and both will pick up passengers from a number of different locations on the west coast. All are out from around 9am until 4pm, apart from the triple-destination tour (roughly 10am–sunset). The circumnavigation cruise costs US$75 per person, Cades Reef US$60, and the triple-destination cruise US$90, all prices including snorkelling gear, a buffet lunch and an open bar. Children under 12 half-price.

Adventure Antigua

☎ 727 3261 or 560 4672,
ⓦ www.adventureantigua.com.
Owner Eli Fuller takes passengers by smallish motorboat on a seven-hour ecotour of the northeast coast of the island, showing where the endangered hawksbill turtles lay their eggs, and

through the mangrove swamps, looking out for rays, frigate birds, osprey and turtles. There are several snorkelling opportunities, and the guide lays on fresh fruit juices, rum punch and lunch on a deserted beach. Cost is US$90 per person, and the trip goes out between two and five times a week, depending on demand.

Jolly Roger Pirate Cruises

T 462 2064,
W www.jollyrogercruises.com.
Hearty party cruises, with rope-swinging and walking the plank for those piratically inclined and limbo competitions and calypso dance classes for the rest. Around US$50 per person.

Kokomo Cats

T 462 7245,
W www.kokomocat.com.
Round the island trips (Tues, Thurs, Sat), Cades Reef (Fri), Great Bird Island (Wed), and a triple destination cruise (Sun) on fast and comfortable catamarans. Kokomo also offer sunset cruises (Tues, Thurs, Sat) from Jolly Harbour on the west coast, out from 6.30–9pm (US$40).

Wadadli Cats

T 462 4792.
Circumnavigation cruises (Thurs, Sat), Cades Reef (Tues), a sunset cruise (Sat US$40), and a triple destination-cruise (Sun).

SAILING

Antigua is one of the prime **sailing** destinations in the Caribbean and, particularly during sailing week in April (see box, opposite), the island becomes a refuelling and party stop for crowds of hearty yachters. If you're after some crewing on boats sailing between the West Indian islands, ask around and look out for crew notices at Nelson's dockyard on the south coast and at the yacht charter outfits (Sun Charters

SAILING WEEK

Begun in 1967 with a tiny fleet of wooden fishing boats, and now regularly graced by over 200 quality yachts, the **English Harbour Race** is the centrepiece of Antigua's sailing week, a festival of racing and partying that transforms the area around Nelson's dockyard into a colourful and crowded carnival village and the harbour into a parking area for every type of sailing boat. Don't expect to find a lot of Antiguans present – its predominantly a party for the American and European sailing contingent – but if you're on the island in late April/early May it's a good place to see some superb sailing action and squeeze in a heavy night of bar-hopping.

and Nicholsons) just outside the dockyard. For information on sailing week and the preceding classic yacht regatta check out their Web sites: Ⓦ www.sailingweek.com and Ⓦ www.antiguaclassics.com.

FISHING

Various charter boats offer **deep-sea fishing trips** where you can go after wahoo, tuna, barracuda and, if you're lucky, marlin and other sailfish. Prices for up to six people start at around US$250 for a half-day, $500 for a whole day, including rods, bait, food, drink and transport from your hotel. If you want to go on your own, operators will put you with another group if they can and charge around US$100 for a half-day. Regular operators include Missa Ferdie (℡ 462 1440), and Overdraft (℡ 462 1961), but if you hunt around at dockside, particularly in St John's and Jolly Harbour, you can find plenty of others.

If you just want to go out with some **local fishermen** – which can be an amazing experience – ask around at one of the main fishing settlements like Old Road on the south coast. Many will be grateful for an extra pair of hands, though you'll need to clarify in advance exactly what's expected of you – pulling lobster pots and fishing nets is extremely tough work and you may be at it for hours.

OTHER WATERSPORTS

Many of the hotels have their own windsurfers which you can borrow for no extra cost, and there's a windsurfing school (daily 9am–5pm) at *Sunsail Colonna* (see p.96) on the northeast coast. Nonguests can buy a day's water-sports pass.

On Dickenson Bay, Sea Sports (☎462 3355) and Pop's (no phone) offer a variety of watersports. A ten-minute parasail costs US$45, a similar period of waterskiing costs US$25, while jet-skis cost US$30 for half an hour (US$40 for a two-seater). If you want to do a lot of watersports, consider buying a day-pass for around US$50 from *Sandals* (see p.95). You'll also find various guys offering you use of their jet-skis and small sailboats at negotiable prices; it usually works out cheaper than going with an established company but bear in mind that insurance will be non-existent.

GOLF

There are two eighteen-hole public **golf courses** in Antigua. Ten-minutes' drive north of St John's, the Cedar Valley Golf Club (☎462 0161) is a 6142-yard, par 70 championship course, venue for the annual Antigua Open, held each November. It's a lovely course, lined with palms, flamboyants and cedars and, from its higher points, offers great panoramic views of the island. Given the dryness of the islands, water hazards are mercifully few but, that aside, it's a reasonably challenging course. Green fees are US$34 for eighteen holes, (US$17 for nine holes), plus US$10 per person for rental of clubs and another US$34 if you want to rent a cart (US$17 for nine holes). The dress code is pretty relaxed, but you will need a collared shirt.

The **Jolly Harbour Golf Course** (℡480 6950) is the island's other major golf location, a 6001-yard, par 71 course designed by American Karl Litten. It's an excellent course, flatter than Cedar Valley but (with seven lakes) more fraught with peril, and it costs around US$50 for eighteen holes.

Barbuda has a tiny course at the *K Club*, but it is open only to guests.

HORSE RIDING

Though you may well be offered a horseback tour during your visit (often, sadly, on a rather mangy and forlorn creature), there is only one official **horse-riding** stable on the island, located just west of Falmouth at Spring Hill (℡460 1775 or 463 8041). They have around a dozen horses and offer lessons for EC$50/US$20 per hour or simple riding tours of the area for EC$40/US$16 per hour.

TENNIS AND SQUASH

Many of the hotels have their own tennis courts, best at places like *Royal Antiguan*, *Rex Halcyon Cove* and the *St James Club*, but there are a handful of public tennis and squash courts available around the island, charging around EC$35/US$14 for an hour, and EC$10/US$4 for hire of equipment.

BBR Sportive
Map 2, C5. Jolly Harbour,
℡462 6260.
Private squash and four floodlit tennis courts at this west-coast resort; rackets and other equipment can be hired.

Temo Sports
Map 5 E4. English Harbour
ⓣ 463 6376.
Squash and synthetic-grass tennis courts, with all equipment available for hire.

BIKING

Cycling is a great way of seeing Antigua, not least because there are few hills and – away from St John's – not much traffic either. Operators offer guided island tours by mountain bike, particularly through attractive places like Fig Tree Drive in the south; if you want to go it alone, several outfits will be happy to rent you a bike.

Cycle Krazy
St John's, ⓣ 462 9253.
Group tours organized with a "support jeep" carrying drinks and first-aid gear. Around US$30 per person for a half-day tour.

Paradise Boat Sales
Jolly Harbour, ⓣ 460 7125, ⓦ www.paradise.com.
Bikes rented for US$15 per day, US$70 for a week.

Shipwreck
St John's, ⓣ 464 7771.
Bikes delivered to your hotel for US$25 for the first day, US$85 for a week.

Tropikelly Trails
Fitches Creek, ⓣ 461 0383, ⓦ www.tropikellytrails.com.
Impressively well-organized tour operator, whose popular guided bike tours – for example down to the south coast – start from St John's and cost US$35 a head including bike, helmet and drinks.

HIKING

There are plenty of great **hikes** in Antigua, a number of them described throughout the Guide (see pp.57, 60, 65 and p.70). For US$20 per person, and assuming they can raise enough hikers to make it worthwhile, Tropikelly Trails (see opposite) organize a pleasant, moderately strenuous two-hour guided tour in the hills of the southwest. More elaborate and longer hikes are periodically organized by Peter Todd of the Hiking Company (☎460 1151) – call to find out what he has planned.

HELICOPTERS

If you want to splash out, Caribbean Helicopters (☎460 5900) offer sightseeing tours for US$75 per person (fifteen-minute, half-island tour) or US$130 (thirty-minute, full-island tour). If there's enough interest, they can also arrange trips to Montserrat for around US$200 per person round-trip.

Directory

All services listed are in St John's unless otherwise stated.

AIRLINES American Airlines ⓣ 462 0952; British Airways ⓣ 462 0876; BWIA ⓣ 480 2942; Carib Aviation ⓣ 462 3147; LIAT ⓣ 480 5600/5610; Virgin ⓣ 560 2079.

AIRPORT DEPARTURE TAX For international flights the departure tax is presently US$20 (EC$50), payable at the airport when you leave.

AMBULANCE Emergency ⓣ 911 or 999; otherwise ⓣ 462 0251.

AMERICAN EXPRESS Rep's office at corner of Long St/Thames St ⓣ 462 4788, open Mon–Thurs 8.30am–4.30pm, Fri 8.30am–5pm.

BANKS St John's: Antigua Commercial Bank, St Mary's/Thames streets (Mon–Thurs 8am–2pm, Fri 8am–5pm); Bank of Antigua, Thames/High streets (Mon–Thurs 8am–3pm, Fri 8am–4pm, Sat 8am–1pm); Barclays, High/Market streets (Mon–Thurs 8am–2pm, Fri 8am–4pm); ABIB, Woods Centre (Mon–Fri 9am–4pm, Sat 9am–1pm). **Nelson's Dockyard**: Bank of Antigua (just inside entrance; Mon–Thurs & Sat 9am–1pm, Fri 9am–noon & 2–4pm).

BOOKSHOPS First Edition, Woods Centre (Mon–Sat 9am–9pm). Excellent place, with the best range of books – including fiction and local interest – in Antigua.

CHILDREN Calm, clear seas, shelving beaches, no serious health risks and a welcoming attitude make Antigua an ideal destination for babies, toddlers and children. Most hotels welcome families and give substantial discounts for children – those under 12 often stay free in their parents' room – but it's worth checking in advance whether they put any restrictions on kids, especially if you're heading for an all-inclusive. You may also want to check on babysitting facilities.

CUSTOMS AND IMMIGRATION The import of weapons and farm produce is heavily restricted, and you'll risk severe penalties if you try to import drugs.

DENTISTS Antigua Barbuda Dental Group, Newgate St ⊤ 460 3368; Dr Maxwell Francis, Cross/Newgate streets ⊤ 462 0058; Dr Sengupta, Woods Centre ⊤ 462 9312.

ELECTRIC CURRENT The island standard is 110 volts with two-pin sockets, though a few of the older hotels still use 220 volts. Take adapters for essential items; some upmarket hotels and guesthouses have them, but you shouldn't count on it.

EMBASSIES British High Commission, 11 Old Parham Rd ⊤ 462 0008; US Consular Agent, Pigeon Point, English Harbour ⊤ 463 6531.

FILM Island Photo, Redcliffe/Market streets, sells film and does one-hour photo development; Benjie's, Heritage Quay, offers the same service and has various camera accessories at duty-free prices.

HOSPITALS Holbertson Public Hospital, Hospital Road ⊤ 462 0251; Adelin Medical Centre, Fort Road ⊤ 462 0866; a new major hospital is slowly being built in St John's at the time of writing, but don't hold your breath.

INTERNET ACCESS There is an Internet café beside the customs office in Nelson's Dockyard and another just outside the dockyard (beside the supermarket next to the *Last Lemming*, see p.122); access is also available at Parcel Post, Redcliffe Quay, St John's. Expect to pay US$3 for 15 minutes.

LAUNDRY Jolly Harbour: Burton's ⊤ 462 7754; **Nelson's**

Dockyard: near the dockyard café, no phone, daily 8am–4pm; **St John's**: Burton's, Independence Drive ⓣ 462 4268.

NEWSPAPERS First Edition at the Woods Centre (Mon–Sat 9am–9pm) gets some US newspapers and the British Sunday papers one day late.

PHARMACIES Full service pharmacies in **St John's**: Benjies, Redcliffe/Market streets ⓣ 462 0733 (Mon–Wed 8.30am–5pm, Thurs & Sat 8.30am–4pm, Fri 8.30am–5.30pm) and Woods, Woods Centre ⓣ 462 9287 (Mon–Sat 9am–10pm, Sun 11am–6pm). **Jolly Harbour**: Woods (Mon–Sat 9am–5.30pm, Sun noon–4pm).

POLICE The main police station is on Newgate St ⓣ 462 0045. Emergency ⓣ 462 0125 or ⓣ 999 or 911.

POST OFFICE **English Harbour**: Mon–Fri 8.30am–4pm; **St John's**: Long St Mon–Fri 8.15am–4pm; Woods Centre Mon–Thurs 8.30am–4pm, Fri 8.30am–5pm.

SUPERMARKETS **English Harbour**: Malones, near Abracadabra, daily 8am–5pm; **Falmouth**: C.E. Bailey, opposite Harbour View Apartments, daily 9am–6pm; **Falmouth Harbour**: Yacht Club Marina, daily 8am–6pm; **Jolly Harbour**: Epicurean, daily 8am–8pm; **St John's**: Woods Centre daily 8am–9pm.

TAXIS West Bus Station Taxis ⓣ 462 5190; Antigua Reliable ⓣ 460 5353.

TELEPHONE Cable & Wireless, St Mary's St, has facilities for making overseas calls.

TIPS AND TAXES Most hotels and restaurants automatically add a service charge of 10 percent and government tax of 7 percent. It's always worth asking if it's included in the quoted price or will be added on later.

TRAVEL AGENTS **English Harbour**: Nicholson's, on the approach to Nelson's Dockyard ⓣ 562 2065 (Mon–Sat 9am–4pm); **St John's**: Bryson's, Long/Thames streets ⓣ 480 1230 (Mon–Fri 8am–4pm, Sat 8am–noon).

DIRECTORY

CONTEXTS

A brief history of Antigua	139
Cricket	147
Books	151

A brief history of Antigua

ntigua's **first people** were the Siboney, originally
from present-day Venezuela in South America, and
the earliest traces of their presence date from around
3100 BC. They were simple, nomadic people who used
flint and shell to make tools and collected fish and conch
from the shallow waters around the islands. By the early
years AD the Siboney had been replaced by Arawak-speak-
ing **Amerindians** from the same region, peaceful, farming
people who made and traded pottery and introduced plants
like cassava, pineapple and tobacco; they in turn were
beginning to be supplanted by the more warlike **Carib**
Indians – who called the island Wadadli – around the time
of Christopher Columbus.

Barbuda's history has taken a somewhat different
course from Antigua's over the last 500 years –
see p.78 for more information.

The first European sighting of Antigua came on
November 11, 1493 when **Columbus**, on his second

voyage of "discovery", sailed close by. He named the island Santa Maria la Antigua after a miracle-working shrine in Seville, where he had prayed before beginning his journey from Spain. Neither Columbus nor his sailors set foot on the heavily wooded island, pressing on instead for the supposed riches to be found further west. In 1525, a small party of Spanish settlers did make it to the island, but harassment from Carib Indians and a shortage of fresh water sources soon drove them off, and the island was left untouched for a century.

In 1624, the first **English settlement** in the West Indies was established on the island of St Kitts, and the English also laid nominal claim to nearby Antigua and Barbuda. Eight years later, a party of English sailors landed on Antigua, founding a settlement at Falmouth on the south coast. These settlers had come to the West Indies to make money from farming, and they experimented with a number of crops – notably tobacco, cotton and indigo – before settling on **sugar**, which was to guarantee the island its future wealth.

Sugarcane was introduced to the Caribbean from Brazil, which supplied eighty percent of the European sugar market during the 1630s. With Brazilian exports disrupted by civil war during the 1640s, an opportunity arose for the West Indian islands – where sugar grew exceptionally well – to feed some of the booming demand for the stuff. Barbados was the first island to seize the opportunity, and Antigua followed soon after with its own mini sugar boom. The population jumped from 750 in 1646 to 1200 a decade later.

Sugar becomes king

By the beginning of the eighteenth century, the Caribs had all been driven off or killed, and sugar was fast becoming king in Antigua. Christopher Codrington's Betty's Hope plantation (see p.55) was a model sugar estate, with all the latest technology, and its success drew more sugar entrepreneurs out from Britain. As they arrived, they cleared their own patch of native forest and the island was gradually denuded of vegetation other than the ubiquitous sugarcane. By 1706 there were 27 sugar mills in Antigua, by 1710 there were 74 and by 1748 there were as many as 175. For 200 years, sugar was to remain far and away the country's dominant industry, bringing enormous wealth to the **planters**, who ran their estates like their personal fiefdoms.

Naturally, other countries looked on this success with envy. Colonial wars between the main European powers were regular events from the mid-seventeenth through to the early nineteenth centuries, and most of Britain's West Indian colonies changed hands as many as a dozen times. Antigua, though, was different in this respect. Although St John's was destroyed by a **French invasion** in 1666, the island never actually fell into French or Dutch hands. This was due, in large part, to the massive fortifications built around it, with forty separate defences erected, the major ones at places like Monks Hill (see p.61) and Shirley Heights (see p.67) on the south coast.

Slavery

The success of the sugar industry, and the wealth of the planters, was of course built upon the appalling inhumanity of **slavery**. Development of the estates required a huge workforce and, with no indigenous population, the only option the planters could envisage was the importation of slaves from Africa, a business that had already been in existence for many years, providing labour throughout the Americas.

SLAVERY

The slave trade was dominated by British merchants. Their ships sailed first to the west coast of Africa – from where most of the slaves were taken – carrying trinkets and other goods to barter for the human cargo. From Africa many of the ships sailed to Jamaica – the most important transhipment point in the region – where the slaves were unloaded into warehouses and sold at auction. The slaves were then sent on to islands like Antigua and Barbados, while the ships would return to Britain, now laden with West Indian products like rum, sugar and spices.

This **triangular trade** brought great riches to the traders, reflected in the development of major British ports like Bristol and Liverpool, but scant attention was paid to the plight of the West Africans. Many were taken prisoner in the heart of their continent, marched hundreds of miles to stockades on the coast and then chained and crammed into the holds of a stinking ship for six to twelve weeks with little room to stretch their limbs, let alone any sanitation facilities. Many died of disease or malnutrition; many others committed suicide if the chance arose, sometimes leaping from the ship rather than continue in captivity.

On arrival in the colonies, the slaves found conditions mostly squalid with little living space or privacy on the sugar estates. Conditions were better in **Barbuda**, where sugar never took hold and slaves worked more as herdsmen and small farmers, but in Antigua the toil of the plantations was relentless, and the whims of the overseers often unimaginably cruel.

Naturally, particularly in the early years, there was **resistance** from the slaves. Runaways fled for the island's woods and the hills around Boggy Peak, but there were few mountainous areas for them to hide and they were easily hunted down. Punishment was swift and brutal. 1736 saw the most serious planning for a slave revolt, with a plot to kill all of the whites in St John's uncovered at the last minute; all of the rebel leaders were executed as a deterrent to those who thought to follow their example. Nonetheless, the plot increased fear among the white population – already massively outnumbered by blacks – and led to increasingly repressive treatment of slaves.

Emancipation

As time went by, conditions for the slaves slowly improved. Religious conversion played a part in this, with Moravian and Methodist **missionaries** coming to Antigua to preach among and help to educate the slaves. Conversion encouraged slave-owners to treat slaves as human for the first time and they even began to give them Sundays off to attend church. In 1807 Britain abolished the slave trade and, in 1834, the Act of Emancipation was passed, and all of the island's 29,000 slaves declared to be free men and women.

Perhaps inevitably, the joy of emancipation soon turned to despair as the freed slaves realized their economic predicament. Unlike Jamaica, which encompassed great tracts of unused land on which former slaves could establish smallholdings, Antigua was almost entirely covered in sugar plantations. Some of the ex-slaves headed for St John's but, with nowhere else to work, many were obliged to continue to labour at the sugar estates and found wages insufficient to provide even the miserly levels of food, housing and care offered under slavery. In particular, the plantation owners no longer felt bound to provide for the very young, the old and the sick, and the numbers of destitute people rose precipitately.

Gradually, though, **free villages** began to emerge at places like Liberta, Jennings and Bendals, often based around Moravian or Methodist churches or on land reluctantly sold by the planters to a group of former slaves. By

1840 there were around thirty such villages, and slowly a few Antiguans scratched together sufficient money to set up their own businesses – shops, taverns and tiny cottage industries. An embryonic black middle class was in the making.

The island's sink into decline

By the mid-nineteenth century the sugar industry was entering a crisis, largely induced by the drop in European sugar prices that followed the introduction of home-produced sugar beet, and aggravated by local droughts and hurricanes. Planters went bankrupt and were forced to sell off their land to local merchants and financial institutions. For a century there was little progress on the island.

By the time of World War II, life for the vast majority of Antiguans was still extremely tough. There was widespread poverty across the island while, for those who did have work on the plantations, hours were long and conditions onerous. In 1938, the **Moyne Commission** was sent from London to report on social conditions in the West Indies, and recorded that Antigua was among the most impoverished and neglected islands in the region. It recommended reform to the island's stringent laws banning trade unions, and in the following year the **Antigua Trades and Labour Union** was formed.

Within a few years the union had helped to improve conditions for plantation workers. Its major success came in 1951 when, under the leadership of former Salvation Army officer **Vere (V.C.) Bird**, workers refused to handle the sugar crop until their rates of pay were improved. For a year, the employers tried to starve the workers into submission, but they were eventually forced to concede a substantial pay rise. National confidence began to improve.

The road to independence

After the war, Antigua continued to be administered from afar by Britain's colonial office, but gradually the island's fledgling politicians were given authority for the day-to-day running of their country. The **Antigua Labour Party** (an offshoot of the ATLU) won the first local **elections** in 1946, and a decade later the island was given responsible ministerial government. Ideological differences between the political parties were minimal, and all parties quickly came to support some sort of independence from Britain. A constitutional conference was held in 1966, leading the following year to autonomy for the country in its internal and foreign affairs, although defence remained a matter for Britain.

Slowly, the national economy began to take strides forward, assisted (despite the closure of the last sugar plantations in 1971) by the development of tourism. By the elections of 1980 all parties considered that, politically and economically, the country was sufficiently mature for full independence and, following a further conference in Britain, the flag of an **independent Antigua and Barbuda** was finally raised in November 1981.

The Bird dynasty

After taking over the leadership of the ATLU in 1943, V.C. Bird dominated Antiguan politics for half a century. Known as Papa Bird, he became the colony's first chief minister in 1956, its first premier in 1967 when internal self-government was granted by Britain, and the first Prime Minister of an independent Antigua and Barbuda in 1981.

Bird (and his entourage) have been consistently controversial. Hugely popular with ordinary Antiguans, he and his government developed a reputation for doing business with all kinds of dodgy characters. There were allegations that ministers had brokered arms deals between Israel and the apartheid regime in South Africa, and even with the Medellin drugs cartel in Colombia. A British commission accused the government of "unbridled corruption", and the USA – who kept a military base on the island and poured in over US$200 million in aid – of turning a blind eye, in an era when fear of radical governments (such as those of Cuba and Grenada) was its leading concern.

Antigua today

Whatever the truth of the allegations, Vere Bird retained power until 1994 when, at the age of 84, he handed leadership of his party and the country to his giant son Lester, once Antigua's leading fast bowler and now probably its wealthiest man. Bird's government has continued to promote tourism (badly dented by a series of hurricanes in the 1990s) as the country's economic dynamo, despite increasing fears for the consequent ecological impact.

Farming (fruit, vegetables and livestock) and light manufacturing continue to provide some diversification for the islands, but a third of the working population are employed by hotels and restaurants, and tourism accounts for about sixty percent of foreign exchange earnings. As a result, Antigua's biggest fear (as with most islands in the region) is that it has put all of its eggs in one basket; should tourism dry up, the country risks being left without any economic lifeline. For now, though, prosperity appears to be still on the rise as the nation begins a new millennium.

Cricket

f you're in Antigua for any length of time, you'll find it almost impossible to avoid the subject of **cricket** – the true national passion. If you're lucky, there'll be a game at the Antigua Recreation Ground in St John's during your stay; if so, don't miss the chance to get along and check out the calypso atmosphere. Failing that, expect at least to get roped into a game of beach cricket, where you'll find fielders standing under the palm trees and in the sea waiting for a miscued shot.

Cricket arrived in Antigua via the British military in the mid-nineteenth century. The 59th Foot Regiment formed the island's first club on New Year's Day 1842, and the *Antigua Times* recorded an Antigua XI beaten by the crew of HMS *Phaeton* at Shirley Heights on September 26, 1863. For decades, cricket clubs remained the preserve of the ruling class: strictly whites-only and often little more than extended social clubs for the planters and merchants. But, despite the early snobbery that was attached to the game, it soon began to catch on in the sugar estates, where the workers drew up their own pitches and organized their own matches.

In 1895 Antigua received its first overseas touring team, who reported playing against a home team composed entirely of "coloured" players. (On the same tour, by comparison,

THE RULES OF CRICKET

The **rules of cricket** are so complex that the official rule book runs to some twenty pages. The basics, however, are by no means as Byzantine as the game's detractors make out.

There are two teams of eleven players. A team wins by scoring more runs than the other team and dismissing all the opposition – in other words, a team could score many runs more than the opposition, but still not win if the last enemy batsman doggedly stays "in" (hence ensuring a draw). The match is divided into innings, when one team bats and the other fields. The number of innings varies depending on the type of competition: one-day matches have one per team, test matches have two.

The aim of the fielding side is to limit the runs scored and get the batsmen "out". Two players from the batting side are on the pitch at any one time. The bowling side has a bowler, a wicketkeeper and nine fielders. Two umpires, one standing behind the stumps at the bowler's end and one square-on to the play, are responsible for adjudicating if a batsman is out. Each innings is divided into overs, consisting of six deliveries, after which the wicketkeeper changes ends, the bowler is changed and the fielders move positions.

the authorities in Barbados excluded black players from their team, irrespective of merit.) In 1920 the Rising Sun Cricket Club was founded for poor men in St John's, and by the 1930s – half a century before independence – Antigua had its first black sporting hero in the batsman **Pat Nanton**.

Nonetheless, Antigua remained a cricketing minnow well into the twentieth century, with the regional game dominated by the "Big Four" cricket nations: Jamaica, Barbados, Trinidad and Guyana. In 1966 the Caribbean Shell Shield

The batsmen score runs either by running up and down from wicket to wicket (one length = one run), or by hitting the ball over the boundary rope, scoring four runs if it crosses the boundary having touched the ground, and six runs if it flies over. The main ways a batsman can be dismissed are: by being "clean bowled", where the bowler dislodges the bails of the wicket (the horizontal pieces of wood resting on top of the stumps); by being "run out", which is when one of the fielding side dislodges the bails with the ball while the batsman is running between the wickets; by being caught, which is when any of the fielding side catches the ball after the batsman has hit it and before it touches the ground; or "LBW" (leg before wicket), where the batsman blocks with his leg a delivery that would otherwise have hit his stumps.

These are the bare rudiments of a game whose beauty lies in the subtlety of its skills and tactics. The captain, for example, chooses which bowler to play and where to position his fielders to counter the strengths of the batsman, the condition of the pitch and a dozen other variables. Cricket also has a beauty in its esoteric language, used to describe such things as fielding positions ("silly mid-off", "cover point", etc) and the various types of bowling delivery ("googly", "yorker", etc).

competition was established for those four and a fifth team – the Combined Islands – made up of players from Antigua and the other small islands. Rarely taken seriously during the 1970s, this Combined Islands team swept to victory in the Shield in 1981, the year of Antigua's independence, led by the brilliant Antiguan **Viv Richards** (see p.46). From that time, the Combined Islands team was allowed to become two – the Leeward Islands of the northeastern Caribbean (dominated by Antigua) and the Windward Islands of the southeast (including Grenada, St Vincent and

CRICKET

St Lucia) – with the Leewards team consistently performing well in both the Shield and the one-day Red Stripe Cup, inaugurated in 1982.

The first Antiguan to play for the West Indies team was fast bowler **Andy Roberts**, who made his debut against England in 1974; he was shortly followed by Richards, who first played against India in the same year. Within a couple of years both players had made a dramatic impact on the side – heavily involved in the slaughter of English cricket in 1976 – and their success lent considerable weight to their country's growing self-confidence in the run-up to independence. In 1981 the island was awarded the right to stage its first test match, where Richards made a superb and entirely predictable century.

Today, unthinkable just two decades ago, tiny Antigua is one of the leading cricketing venues in the Caribbean, with test matches, Busta Cup and Red Stripe Cup games played there annually. Between 1985 and 1995 the West Indies team was captained by Antiguans – Richards and, later, his protégé Richie Richardson – and Antiguan players like wicketkeeper Ridley Jacobs continue to feature prominently in the side. Small wonder, perhaps, that at times people appear to talk of little else.

CRICKET

Books

Several of the harder to find books described below are available at the national museum in St John's (see p.45).

History

Reynolds Morse, *The Quest for M.P. Shiel's Realm of Redonda* (Cleveland). The bizarre story of the kings of uninhabited Redonda (see p.86).

Desmond Nicholson, *Antigua, Barbuda & Redonda – a Historical Sketch*; *Forts of Antigua & Barbuda*; *The Story of the Arawaks* (all Museum of Antigua and Barbuda). Superbly researched studies of the island by Antigua's leading historian.

J.P. Parry, Philip Sherlock and Anthony Maingot, *A short history of the West Indies* (Macmillan). The best concise history of the region, taking the story up to the mid-1980s and good on general issues like regional co-operation and debt crisis.

Biography and memoir

Vincent Harlow, *Christopher Codrington 1669–1710* (Oxford University Press). Not easy to get hold of, but a fascinating biography of Antigua's first sugar-baron, who was also the "founder" of Barbuda.

Jamaica Kincaid, *A Small Place* (Vintage). A scathing work by Antigua's most famous and

A SMALL PLACE

Savage and satirical, *A Small Place* is author **Jamaica Kincaid's** polemic on the corruption of her country at the hands of its colonial and present-day rulers. Don't expect to find the book in Antigua; its sale is banned to avoid distress to the venal politicians and patronizing tourists who draw equal fire from her pen. Barbed as it is, though, the book makes for an invigorating and provocative read, the complaint of a small girl who lived on a street named after an English "maritime criminal" (Nelson) and grew up to see roads being repaired for the visit of the queen from England, and government ministers flying off for medical treatment in New York while the Antiguan hospitals were left understaffed and underfunded.

Now available!

now self-exiled novelist (see box, above).

Patrick Leigh Fermor, *The Traveller's Tree* (Penguin). The classic Caribbean travelogue describing the author's visit in the 1940s, before tourism had really started in the region, though only one of the chapters covers his time on Antigua.

Viv Richards and Bob Harris, *Sir Vivian* (Penguin). Excellent autobiography of Antigua's finest cricketer.

Keithlyn Smith and Fernando Smith, *To Shoot Hard Labour (the Life and Times of Samuel Smith, an Antiguan Workingman)* (Karia Press). Graphic and often poignant account of life in Antigua during and after slavery.

Literature

Gisele Isaac, *Considering Venus* (Seaburn). First novel by the writer of the first Antiguan movie, *The Sweetest Mango* (see p.121), exploring the issue of lesbianism between Caribbean women and set between Antigua – where the author grew up – and New York, where she worked and taught.

George Lamming, *In the Castle of my Skin* (Longman).

E

eating and drinking 103–117
embassies 20, 135
English Harbour 62

F

Falmouth 59
festivals...31
Fig Tree Hill 72
film 135
fishing...129
Fitches Creek 54
Five Islands...................................75
flights
    from Australia and New Zealand 12
    from Britain and Ireland 4
    from the US and Canada 8
    to Barbuda 80
    to neighbouring islands 28
Fort Barrington 76
Fort Bay 48
Fort Berkeley 66
Fort James 48
frigate birds..................................82

G

getting around 15–19
golf 130
Great Fort George...........................61
Green Castle Hill 75
Green Island 56

H

Half Moon Bay 57
harassment....................................34
Harmony Hall 56
Hawksbill Bay 76
health 21
helicopter rides 133
hiking 57, 60, 65, 70, 133
history 139–146

horse riding 131
hospitals 135

I

Indian Creek 70
information 24–26
insurance 22
Internet 135
Island Arts Gallery 53

J

Jolly Harbour 74

K

Kincaid, Jamaica.........................152

L

laundry 135
Liberta 71
Long Bay 56

M

Mamora Bay 70
money 26
Monk's Hill 61
motorbikes 17
music 118–122

N

Nanton, Pat 148
Nelson's Dockyard 62–66
newspapers 30, 136
nightlife 118–122

O

Old Road 73

P

Parham 54
pharmacies 136
Pigeon Beach 67
police 136
post office 29, 136

R

radio 30
Redonda 86
Rendezvous Bay 60
Richards, Viv 46, 149
Roberts, Andy 150
Runaway Bay 52

S

sailing 128
Sailing Week 129
St George's Parish Church 54
St John's 39–50
    accommodation 90
    cathedral 46
    Coates Cottage 43
    eating 105
    getting around 40
    Heritage Quay 43
    history 41
    information 40
    market 47
    National Museum 45
    Recreation Ground 44
    Redcliffe Quay 42
    shopping 49
St Paul's Church 60
St Peter's Parish Church 54

St Stephen's Anglican Church 55
scooters 17
scuba diving 124
Shirley Heights 67–70
shopping 33, 49
snorkelling 125
sports 123–133
squash 131
supermarket 136
Sweetest Mango, The 121
Swetes 72

T

taxes 136
taxis 17, 136
telephone 29, 136
tennis 131
tipping 136
tours 18
travel agents 136
traveller's cheques 27
Turner's Beach 74

U

Urlings 74

V

visas 19

W

weather xi
Web sites 25

MUSIC ROUGH GUIDES on CD

YOUR GUIDES TO A WORLD OF MUSIC

'Rough Guides have long been noted for their
excellent travel books. Take note, because their
musical guides are equally thorough and
enjoyable' *HMV Choice (UK)*

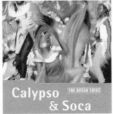

Available from book and record shops worldwide or order direct from
World Music Network, Unit 6, 88 Clapham Park Road, London SW4 7BX
tel: 020 7498 5252 • fax: 020 7498 5353 • email: post@worldmusic.net

Hear samples from over 70 Rough Guide CDs at

WWW.WORLDMUSIC.NET

Visit us online
roughguides.com

Information on over 25,000 destinations around the world

- **Read** Rough Guides' trusted travel info
- **Share** journals, photos and travel advice with other readers
- Get exclusive Rough Guide **discounts** and travel **deals**
- Earn membership points every time you contribute to the Rough Guide **community** and get **free** books, flights and trips
- Browse thousands of CD reviews and artists in our **music** area

Will you have enough stories to tell your grandchildren?

© 2000 Yahoo! Inc.

Yahoo! Travel

Do You YAHOO!?

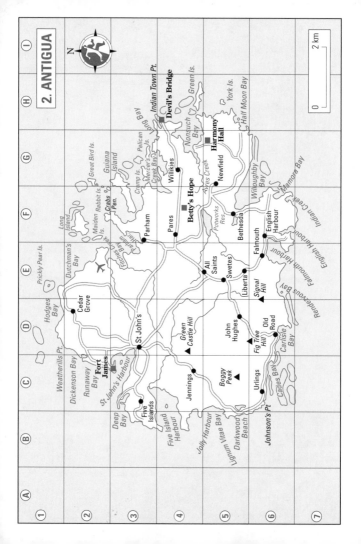

2. ANTIGUA

N

0   2 km

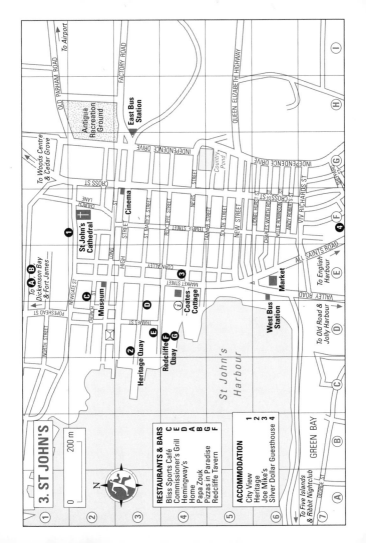

3. ST JOHN'S

0   200 m

N

RESTAURANTS & BARS
Bliss Sports Café   C
Commissioner's Grill   E
Hemingway's   D
Home   A
Papa Zouk   B
Pizzas in Paradise   G
Redcliffe Tavern   F

ACCOMMODATION
City View   1
Heritage   2
Joe Mike's   3
Silver Dollar Guesthouse   4

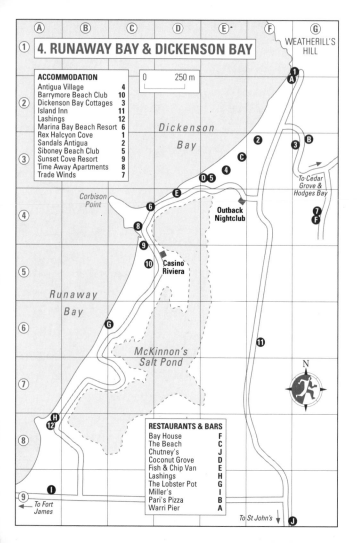

4. RUNAWAY BAY & DICKENSON BAY

WEATHERILL'S HILL

ACCOMMODATION

Antigua Village	4
Barrymore Beach Club	10
Dickenson Bay Cottages	3
Island Inn	11
Lashings	12
Marina Bay Beach Resort	6
Rex Halcyon Cove	1
Sandals Antigua	2
Siboney Beach Club	5
Sunset Cove Resort	9
Time Away Apartments	8
Trade Winds	7

0   250 m

Dickenson Bay

To Cedar Grove & Hodges Bay

Corbison Point

Outback Nightclub

Casino Riviera

Runaway Bay

McKinnon's Salt Pond

N

RESTAURANTS & BARS

Bay House	F
The Beach	C
Chutney's	J
Coconut Grove	D
Fish & Chip Van	E
Lashings	H
The Lobster Pot	G
Miller's	I
Pari's Pizza	B
Warri Pier	A

To Fort James

To St John's

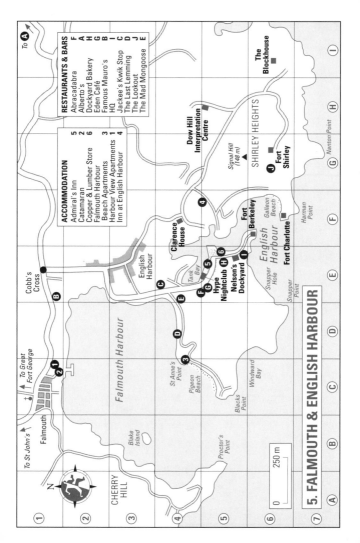

RESTAURANTS & BARS

Abracadabra	F
Alberto's	A
Dockyard Bakery	H
Eden Café	G
Famous Mauro's	B
HQ	I
Jackee's Kwik Stop	C
The Last Lemming	D
The Lookout	J
The Mad Mongoose	E

ACCOMMODATION

Admiral's Inn	5
Catamaran	2
Copper & Lumber Store	6
Falmouth Harbour Beach Apartments	3
Harbour View Apartments	1
Inn at English Harbour	4

To St John's
To Great Fort George
To A

Falmouth
Cobb's Cross
English Harbour
Clarence House
Dow Hill Interpretation Centre
Signal Hill (148 m)
SHIRLEY HEIGHTS
Fort Shirley
The Blockhouse

Falmouth Harbour
CHERRY HILL
Blake Island
Proctor's Point
St Anne's Point
Pigeon Beach
Blacks Point
Windward Bay
Tank Bay
Hype Nightclub
Nelson's Dockyard
Fort Berkeley
Galleon Beach
English Harbour
Fort Charlotte
Snapper Hole
Harman Point
Snapper Point
Nanton Point

N

0   250 m

5. FALMOUTH & ENGLISH HARBOUR

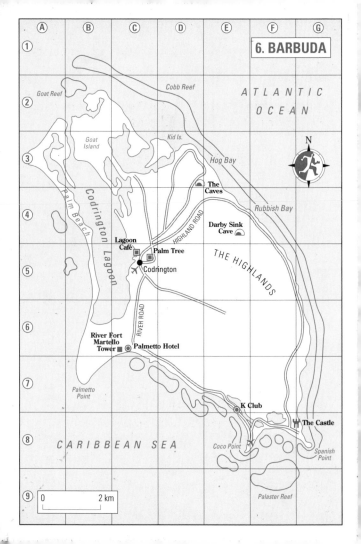

6. BARBUDA

	(A)	(B)	(C)	(D)	(E)	(F)	(G)

ATLANTIC OCEAN

Goat Reef

Cobb Reef

Goat Island

Kid Is.

Hog Bay

Palm Beach

Codrington Lagoon

The Caves

Rubbish Bay

Darby Sink Cave

HIGHLAND ROAD

Lagoon Café

Palm Tree

Codrington

THE HIGHLANDS

N

RIVER ROAD

River Fort Martello Tower

Palmetto Hotel

Palmetto Point

K Club

The Castle

CARIBBEAN SEA

Coco Point

Spanish Point

Palaster Reef

0   2 km